When They Began to

Sing

UNDERSTANDING GOD'S PURPOSE
FOR THE MUSIC MINISTRY

LEGACY
PUBLISHERS INTERNATIONAL

When They Began to

Sing

UNDERSTANDING GOD'S PURPOSE
FOR THE MUSIC MINISTRY

Alvin D. Fruga

WHEN THEY BEGAN TO SING: Understanding God's Purpose for the Music Ministry

ISBN 1-880809-54-0

Printed in the United States of America

Copyright © 2005 by Alvin D. Fruga

Legacy Publishers International
1301 South Clinton Street
Denver, CO 80247
Phone: 303-283-7480 FAX: 303-283-7536

Library of Congress Cataloging-in-Publication Data Pending

1 2 3 4 5 6 7 8 9 10 / 10 09 08 07 06 05

Dedication

This book is dedicated to the memory of my mother, Joyce A. Fruga.

My mom had a chance to read the first draft of this book long before she went to heaven. She was very excited that one of her children was actually writing a book.

My mother always encouraged me to go after my dreams, and she also taught me the importance of humility before God and man. She was anointed to touch people's lives, and she always did it with a smile. Her legacy of love, creativity, and the unwavering pursuit of fulfilling one's God-given destiny while on this earth lives on through the lives of her four children.

Acknowledgments

—◆◆◆◆◆—

I want to thank Michele Leonard and the entire Legacy Publishers International family for taking my vision and running with it. You are truly a Godsend.

Special thanks to my three siblings and their spouses: my sister, Jeanice Williams, and her husband Jack; my elder brother, Willie Fruga, Jr., and his wife Sandra; and my younger, but taller, brother, DeJon Fruga, and his wife Christina. Your constant love and prayer support has been a tremendous blessing to Sennola and me. We love you!

To my dad, Willie Fruga, Sr., who taught me how to play the piano at a young age. You inspired me into the music ministry by allowing me to "hang out" with you at choir rehearsals and church services. Thanks, Dad!

Love and honor to my childhood sweetheart and best friend, my beautiful wife, Sennola, who never ceases to support me in all my ministry endeavors. You are truly SENNOLARRIFIC!

And to my four priceless gifts, my children, Michael, Teree, Kambri, and Shannon, for always reminding me that ministry begins at home. Superdad loves you.

Contents

WHEN THEY BEGAN TO SING

And when they began to sing and to praise, the LORD set ambushments against the children of Ammon, Moab, and mount Seir, which were come against Judah; and they were smitten.

2 Chronicles 20:22, KJV

Introduction

"Daddy, can I go with you to choir rehearsal tonight?" I can remember asking my father this question every week during most of my childhood. As a young boy fascinated by music, I loved going to choir rehearsal with my dad, not just to hear the choir sing, although that was a part of it; but more importantly, to see him in action. He was not just a choir member; he was the music director.

I can remember sitting on the edge of my seat in choir rehearsals and church services, watching my dad teach, direct, and motivate both singers and musicians to the point that they would give absolutely everything they had musically and spiritually in praise to the Lord. Of course, I said, as most boys do, "I want to be just like my dad."

It was amazing to me how he could, with seemingly little effort, teach all the choir parts, from soprano to bass. My dad was also an accomplished musician. He knew exactly what each band member was supposed to play and when. He had such a confident command of everything that was taking place musically with a church service. Yes, I definitely wanted to be a chip off the old block.

No wonder it was such an easy transition for me, when I became a teenager, to go from being on the sidelines to actually singing in the church choir. I still remember the awesome feeling of standing in front of the congregation for the first time as a choir member. I would never be the same again. The many things I learned musically and the friendships I developed are experiences I will never forget.

I can even remember singing in my first choir concert: black pants, white shirt, black tie, and eyes bugged out wide with uncontrollable excitement. I had to stand in the front row of the tenor section because I was so short. I've grown a little since then, and I no longer have those particular black pants, shirt, or tie, but I still haven't figured out how to control my eyes.

I have fond memories of long choir trips to other churches. We would sing an entire concert for the bus driver before we ever arrived at our destination. I remember going to choir fellowships at a member's home. We would have a great time eating, laughing at things that happened in church, eating again, playing games, eating, and, of course, singing. We always sang. Well, it wasn't long before I was directing choirs myself. I was doing exactly what I had observed my father do for years.

As a musician, I spent countless hours teaching, directing, and yes, even motivating singers and musicians. I eventually realized that music ministry was my calling, and I would be involved in that area of ministry the rest of my life. This revelation of my call, along with the desire to give God my very best, caused me to ask some very important questions. How did the music ministry originate? And why? What is the purpose for music in the church?

All right, I'll be very honest with you. After being a choir member for years, and subsequently a music director, I realized I didn't really understand the spiritual significance behind all the music. Oh yes, I knew I was giving glory to God, and I knew He had called me to the music ministry. But I honestly didn't know God's original intent and purpose for music in the church. All I knew was that music helped to make the service flow better, providing a sort of Christian entertainment for the congregation.

Now, you be honest with me, and with yourself. Do you know God's purpose for music in the church? Do you have a clear understanding of what was in His heart when He first instituted this ministry? I submit to you that the music ministry serves a much more meaningful purpose than simply filling space in a service or providing some type of entertainment for the congregation. There is a specific spiritual role that music plays in a service, which can be traced back to its origin in scripture.

The Lord has shared with me some exciting truths regarding the music ministry, and they have totally revolutionized my thinking and sharpened my spiritual focus during church services. I thank God that I not only know what I'm doing; I now also know why I'm doing it.

It is for this reason that I have written this book. I have a deep concern for pastors, music directors, choir members, and congregational members who may not fully understand the purpose for the music ministry. Many of us understand the musical aspects, but not the spiritual aspects.

What spiritual purpose does music serve in the church? What actually takes place in the Spirit realm when we sing praises to God? Why does the enemy try so hard to come against the infrastructure of our music programs, doing all he can to create division and disunity? Why is the music ministry such a threat to him? If we who are involved in music ministry don't know the answers to these questions, we can never be totally effective in our call.

Introduction

Music plays a vital role within a church service. Although nothing can take the place of the spoken Word of God, the music ministry is very significant, simply because it prepares the congregation to receive the Word. The singing of a choir, accompanied by musicians, can easily be compared to the ministry of John the Baptist, in that it is the voice of one crying in the wilderness, *"Prepare ye the way of the Lord"* (Luke 3:4, KJV). A choir singing in unity is one voice crying out in worship to the Lord.

The mission of singers and musicians is to prepare, repair, recondition, and purify the spiritual atmosphere in order for the Word of God to fall on good ground. Music sets the atmosphere and paves the way for the congregation to receive the Word and, ultimately, to be set free.

It is not the pastor's responsibility to do this. The path should already be cleared when he or she gets up to speak. The pastor should be totally free to minister the Word, and the congregation should be ready to receive the Word without any hindrances or distractions.

This is the reason for Satan's many attacks on the music ministry. He knows that if the congregation receives the truth, they will be set free and live more victoriously.

It is my desire to expose this deception of the enemy, and also to reveal and release God's truth concerning the music ministry, so that we can begin to experience some of the same results as the children of Israel *"when they began to sing."* Whether you're a pastor, music director, musician, choir member, or parishioner, my prayer is that through this book you may gain a fresh and renewed understanding of God's purpose for the music ministry, and that you will take the necessary steps to insure that the music program in your church is fulfilling its purpose.

It's been many years now since the time I asked my dad to take me to choir rehearsals with him. I can still hear those words loud and clear, "Daddy, can I go with you to choir rehearsal tonight?" Only now, it's my children asking me.

Alvin D. Fruga
Fort Worth, Texas

Chapter 1

The Biblical History of the Music Ministry

—✦✧✦✧✦—

The first step to gaining a better understanding of God's purpose for the music ministry is to take a look back into biblical history and see how, when, and why it originated. This will give us invaluable insight as to what the purpose of our music programs should be today. As you embark on this exciting musical journey into God's Word, He will unveil some of the most wonderful truths regarding the music ministry that you've ever known.

Moses' Era

The history of music in the Jewish temple dates from Moses' day, between 1300 to 1200 B.C., and it centered around the care of and worship in what was called the Tent of Meeting, the place where the Israelites often met with God. The very foundation and purpose for music in the Church was definitely established during this period, as recorded in the book of Exodus.

In Exodus chapter 32, Moses had been up on Mt. Sinai for forty days and forty nights, talking to God and receiving the Law and commandments from Him written on tablets of stone. The children of Israel had just entered into a covenant with God to worship and obey Him only, but now they became impatient with Moses and with God, and, with the help of Aaron, Moses' brother, they decided to make their own god. They melted down their gold earrings, and fashioned the resulting gold into the form of a golden calf. Then they sacrificed burnt offerings to this god, and worshiped it with singing and dancing. As a result of the Israelites' corruption, God sent Moses back down from Mt. Sinai to deal with their sinful acts:

> And the LORD said unto Moses, Go, get thee down; for thy people, which thou broughtest out of the land of Egypt, have corrupted themselves.
>
> Exodus 32:7, KJV

Notice here that God was already disturbed with the children of Israel by the way He referred to them. He now addressed them as Moses' people, whom Moses had brought out of Egypt, rather than His people whom

2

He had brought out of Egypt. In fact, if it hadn't been for Moses pleading the Israelites' case, God would have totally destroyed them all then and there (see verses 9-14). What a great example of God's mercy toward His people! Although He chastised them, He did not utterly destroy them.

As Moses and Joshua came down from the mountain, they heard a noise, which Joshua described as a sound of war. Moses disagreed with this description. This was not a sound of war, because the noise was neither a cry of defeat, nor a cry of victory (see verses 15-18). Moses described it as *"the noise of them that sing"* (verse 18, KJV). It was apparently a familiar sound to Moses, because he was able to distinguish what it was. How did he know?

Very little information is given to us concerning Moses' childhood. Except for the fact that he was born a Hebrew and raised as an Egyptian, we know very little about his growing up years. But one could suggest, from Exodus 2:11, that Moses often went to the place where his own people were working to watch them. Perhaps he heard them singing there, for this was definitely a sound that Moses had heard many times before.

Unfortunately, the particular singing by the Israelites that Moses and Joshua heard that day was to the wrong god. In just forty-two days, they had already broken their covenant with the true and living God, and, once again, had resorted to idolatry.

As Moses reached the edge of the camp, he saw firsthand the idolatry of God's people and he became very angry. He broke the tablets of stone as an outward sign of Israel's broken covenant with God (see verse 19). He also burned the golden calf, ground it into powder, mixed the powder with water, and made the Israelites drink the mixture (see verse 20).

But that wasn't all Moses did. After giving Aaron a stiff talking to, Moses realized that the people were naked and had shamed themselves before their enemies. It was at this time that Moses asked one of the most important and pivotal questions in the history of all mankind:

Who is on the LORD's side? Let him come unto me.

Exodus 32:26, KJV

Of the twelve tribes of Israel, only one tribe responded positively to Moses' question that day. Without hesitation, the Levites came to where Moses was.

I'm sure this pleased Moses, because he was from the tribe of Levi himself. Of more significance, however, is the fact that it pleased God. Of all the twelve tribes of Israel, the Levites were the only tribe to realize their mistakes and return to the Lord. This response by the Levites so moved God's heart that He chose them to be the only tribe to work and minister in His temple. They would perform these religious duties in the future on behalf of all of Israel.

> *The LORD said to Moses, "Bring the tribe of Levi and present them to Aaron the priest to assist him. They are to perform duties for him and for the whole community at the Tent of Meeting by doing the work of the tabernacle. They are to take care of all the furnishings of the Tent of Meeting, fulfilling the obligations of the Israelites by doing the work of the tabernacle. Give the Levites to Aaron and his sons; they are the Israelites who are to be given wholly to him. Appoint Aaron and his sons to serve as priests; anyone else who approaches the sanctuary must be put to death."*
>
> Numbers 3:5-10

God didn't stop there. He wanted all Israel to know that the Levites were now His. So He replaced all the firstborn males of Israel, which He had previously set aside for Himself, with the tribe of Levi.

> *The LORD also said to Moses, "I have taken the Levites from among the Israelites in place of the first male offspring of every Israelite woman. The Levites are mine, for all the firstborn are mine. When I struck down all the firstborn in Egypt, I set apart for myself every firstborn in Israel,*

whether man or animal. They are to be mine. I am the LORD."

Numbers 3:11-13

By doing this, God established the Levites as His eternal firstborn. The Levites were a constant reminder to God that if no other tribe worshiped Him, they would. They became God's personal praise remnant. As a result, God would not allow anyone but the Levites to minister in or around the place where He dwelt.

The Levites were set aside for the express purpose of caring for the sanctuary and ministering before the Lord. Their initial duties included transporting the tabernacle and its furniture whenever the camp was moved. This included the Ark of the Covenant, which represented the very presence of God among the Israelites. They would also set up the Tent of Meeting and thoroughly clean and care for it day and night.

The Levites also assisted the priests who were under Aaron's leadership at that time. Other duties included doorkeeper, temple musician, and administrator.

God wanted to make it very clear that the Levites were to be His chosen ones to care for and minister in the Tent of Meeting. In order to accomplish this, He set them apart from the rest of the Israelites:

The LORD said to Moses: "Take the Levites from among the other Israelites and make them ceremonially clean."

Numbers 8:5-6

God wanted them separated from the rest of the tribes of Israel, and He even wanted them cleaner than the rest of the tribes of Israel. Therefore, He took them through a special purification process. From this day onward there would be distinct differences between the Levites and the rest of the tribes.

Only the Levites, along with Aaron and his sons, would offer atonement for sin, thus serving as an Old Testament advocate on behalf of all Israel. The Levites were so special to God that He gave them as a gift to Aaron, the priest, for this specific purpose:

Of all the Israelites, I have given the Levites as gifts to Aaron and his sons to do the work at the Tent of Meeting on behalf of the Israelites and to make atonement for them so that no plague will strike the Israelites when they go near the sanctuary.

Numbers 8:19

God also gave them as a gift to ensure that the temple was properly and constantly cared for:

I myself have selected your fellow Levites from among the Israelites as a gift to you, dedicated to the Lord to do the work at the Tent of Meeting.

Numbers 18:6

I really like the use of the word *"gift"* in these passages, because it demonstrates God's love and concern for His Church, and the priest, or pastor, who has given his life to oversee the temple. God saw that Aaron needed help in the house of the Lord, so He gave him a *"gift."* This *"gift"* came in the form of tent custodians, gatekeepers, administrators, and, yes, musicians and singers. The music ministry is a *"gift"* from God to pastors and their churches, in order to assist them in the work of the ministry.

God also provided a source of payment for those who worked in the temple. The Levites would not be given an inheritance, like the other tribes of Israel. They would, instead, receive the tithe from the other eleven tribes of Israel as their inheritance.

"I give to the Levites all the tithes in Israel as their inheritance in return for the work they do while serving at the Tent of Meeting. From now on the Israelites must not go near the Tent of Meeting, or they will bear the consequences of their sin and will die. It is the Levites who are to do the work at the Tent of Meeting and bear the responsibility for offenses against it. This is a lasting ordinance for the generations to come. They will receive no inheritance among the

Israelites. Instead, I give to the Levites as their inheritance the tithes that the Israelites present as an offering to the LORD. That is why I said concerning them: 'They will have no inheritance among the Israelites.'"

Numbers 18:21-24

This gives more than adequate biblical support for paying workers in the church today, including musicians and singers. Most churches today at least pay their music director and musicians, but one might suggest that a church could go bankrupt if it also paid every choir member. I strongly disagree. Most churches simply suffer from improper giving habits.

For example, in most churches today, only about twenty percent of the congregation supports eighty percent of the entire church budget. In other words, eighty percent of the members of most congregations give only enough to cover twenty percent of the church expenses. As a result, we're not in the financial position to bless every person who gives their time in service to the Lord.

Most choir members never think about getting paid and might even take offense to being offered payment for something they love to do, and the ones who demand payment for their services need to recheck their motives. But the point I'm making here is that most churches today have missed the perfect

WHEN THEY BEGAN TO SING

plan of God as it relates to His provision for all temple workers.

In many cases, we have totally dismissed the idea of actually paying those who work in the temple, on the grounds that it's financially unfeasible, when in fact we have failed to properly teach our congregations God's all-inclusive purpose for the tithe. For the Levites, their ministry in the temple was their livelihood. They didn't have another job outside their work in the temple:

> *And these are the singers, chief of the fathers of the Levites, who remaining in the chambers were free: for they were employed in that work day and night.*
>
> 1 Chronicles 9:33, KJV

There was no question as to what God wanted and required. All of Israel would tithe, and that tithe would go to all those who worked in the temple.

Giving the tithe was not an option; it was a command. The question is: has God changed His commands? I don't think so. What we must do is allow the truth of God's Word concerning tithing to set us free from the lies with which Satan has seemingly tricked us. When all of God's people learn the importance of tithing and begin to financially operate solely based on His truth, the entire Body of Christ, including the area of music, will experience a mighty move of God.

When Moses asked, *"Who is on the Lord's side?"*, the Levites realized their error, repented of worshiping the golden image, and returned to the Lord. As a result, God chose them to be the only ones who could minister to Him in the Tent of Meeting. This marks the beginning of what we know today as music ministry within the Church.

We can learn a lot from the Levites. They were by no means perfect. The only thing that separated them from the other host of idolaters was that they realized their mistakes and returned to the Lord. True servants of God are those who, no matter what mistakes they make, will always find their way back to the bosom of the Father.

King David's Era

It wasn't until about 1000 B.C., during the period of the kings of Israel, that a more distinct role for music in the temple was seen. The first choirs actually mentioned in the Bible appear during the reign of King David. This is not at all surprising, since David had been an accomplished musician, singer, and songwriter from his youth.

My favorite account of David was when he played the harp for King Saul. Not only was King Saul refreshed, but an evil spirit left him as a result of David's ministry (see 1 Samuel 16:23). This alone is evidence enough to prove that God desires for music to minister healing and deliverance to those in need.

When David became king, one of the first things he did was to return the Ark of the Lord to its proper place in Jerusalem. The Ark of the Covenant represented the very presence of God among the children of Israel. It was the only article of furniture within the Temple of Meeting which was placed in the Holy of Holies. Only the high priest could enter this innermost room of the temple, and he could go in only once a year, to offer an atonement for the sin for all Israel.

The Ark had a gold cover which was called the Mercy Seat. The Israelites believed that this was the very throne of God. The Ark was so sacred that whenever the Israelites moved their camp to a new location, the Levites, by God's order, were the only ones who could carry the Ark. The presence of the Ark among the Israelites was also a sign to them of God's approval and provision.

The Ark was, however, not always in the Israelites' camp. The Israelites were, at one time, defeated by the Philistines, who captured the Ark from them (see 1 Samuel 4:1-11). Then, however, disaster hit the camp of the Philistines because of their mishandling of the Ark. It wasn't long before the Philistines sent it back (see 1 Samuel 5 and 6). The Ark ended up in a place called Kiriath Jearim.

So the men of Kiriath Jearim came and took up the ark of the LORD. They took it to Abinadab's house on the hill and consecrated Eleazar his son to guard the ark of the LORD. It was a long time, twenty years in all, that the ark remained at Kiriath Jearim, and all the people of Israel mourned and sought after the LORD.

1 Samuel 7:1-2

During this twenty-year period, which occurred during the reign of King Saul and the exile of David, the future king, the children of Israel were without the Ark in Jerusalem, and thus felt like they did not have God's presence, or approval, among them. But when David became king, he immediately took action to bring the Ark back to its rightful place:

David conferred with each of his officers, the commanders of thousands and commanders of hundreds. He then said to the whole assembly of Israel, "If it seems good to you and if it is the will of the LORD our God, let us send word far and wide to the rest of our brothers throughout the territories of Israel, and also the priests and Levites who are with them in their towns and pasturelands, to come and join us. Let us bring the ark of our God back to us, for we did not inquire of it during the reign of Saul." The whole assembly agreed to do this, because it seemed right to all the people.

1 Chronicles 13:1-4

David specifically asked for the priests and Levites from the various surrounding regions of Israel to come and join in the celebration of bringing the Ark back to Jerusalem. But for some reason he allowed Abinadab's sons, Uzzah and Ahio, to guide the cart which carried the Ark. In this, he made two costly mistakes.

First, the Ark should not have been placed on a cart. God had specifically chosen the Levites to carry it. They were to carry it on their shoulders using the poles that slid underneath the base of the Ark, making sure never to actually touch it. This was one of their prescribed duties.

Secondly, Uzzah and Ahio were not Levites. They were from the tribe of Judah. Only the Levites were to be in close proximity to the Ark.

In addition to these mistakes, Uzzah committed another deadly error. He reached out and touched the Ark in order to steady it. This was all that God could take. No one, not even the Levites, were to ever touch the Ark. In that moment, God struck Uzzah dead, and the entire procession came to a standstill.

The singing stopped, the music stopped, and the dancing stopped. There comes a time in our praise and worship and choir singing when various aspects of our celebration are critically wrong. It's at these times that we must be willing to stop the music until

things are corrected. We will discuss this important truth further in Chapter 5.

The reason many of our music programs lack the approval of God and sometimes even suffer spiritual defeat is because the wrong people are handling the Ark. As stated before, Ahio and Uzzah were from the tribe of Judah, which translated in Hebrew means *"praise."* [1] But, as proven by Uzzah, it's not good enough for singers and musicians to have only a spirit of praise (Judah); they must be of the tribe and spirit of Levi.

The name Levi, as translated in Hebrew, means "to be attached, to twine, to unite, to remain, to join or be joined." [2] This suggests that even in times of great temptation and distress, the true Levites will always return, or join, themselves to God. There is a divine connection between God and that Levitical spirit. Anybody can praise God, but only Levites can handle, or carry, the anointing.

As a result of King David's error and Uzzah's death, the Ark did not make it to Jerusalem at that time. It ended up at Obed-Edom's house, where it remained for the next three months (see 1 Chronicles 13:12-14).

Then King David, realizing his costly mistakes, decided to try once again to bring the Ark back to Jerusalem. This time he would do it the way God had originally instructed. He assembled the Levites and gave them specific instructions:

15

He said to them, "You are the heads of the Levitical families; you and your fellow Levites are to consecrate yourselves and bring up the ark of the LORD, the God of Israel, to the place I have prepared for it. It was because you, the Levites, did not bring it up the first time that the LORD our God broke out in anger against us. We did not inquire of him about how to do it in the prescribed way."

1 Chronicles 15:12-13

This last sentence of verse 13 is very powerful! We can save ourselves a lot of unnecessary trouble and distress by taking the time to seek the Lord as to how we should bring His presence into the temple.

The Levites consecrated themselves *"in order to bring up the ark of the Lord"* (verse 14). Then they carried the Ark with the poles on their shoulders. In other words, after the Levites consecrated themselves, they were free to allow the presence of God to rest on them. Selah!

In verse 16 of this same chapter, we see the first organized choir and orchestra, along with a minister of music. David wanted to make sure that there would be singing and rejoicing taking place while the Ark was being carried. So he appointed specific singers and musicians from among the Levites to perform these duties.

David told the leaders of the Levites to appoint their brothers as singers to sing joyful songs, accompanied by musical instruments: lyres, harps and cymbals.

1 Chronicles 15:16

This is the first biblical account of an organized music ministry, and all of the musicians and singers were Levites. The rest of this chapter describes exactly who performed what duties.

According to Genesis 46:11 and 1 Chronicles 6:1, Levi, the father of the Levites, had three sons. Their names are Gershon, Kohath, and Merari. In 1 Chronicles 6:31-46, a description is given as to who, from among these three sons of Levi, were actually leaders involved in the ministry of music. From the descendants of Levi's middle son Kohath, Heman was chosen. From the descendants of Levi's oldest son Gershon, Asaph was chosen. And from the descendants of Levi's youngest son Merari, Ethan was chosen.

Taking this into account, we can better understand the family roots of the Levites mentioned in 1 Chronicles 15:17 and following. The Tribe of Levi Flow Chart on page 18 shows Levi's three sons and their descendants, from which came the head musicians and singers.

Heman, Asaph, and Ethan were all musicians according to 1 Chronicles 15:19. Although they were

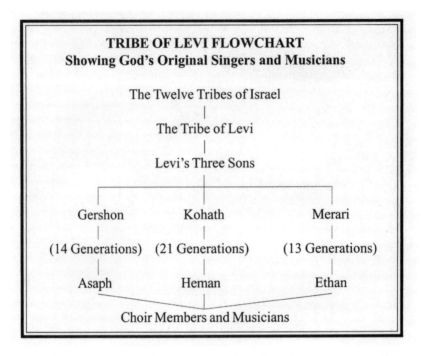

cymbal players, they were also leaders among the musicians. It was Chenaniah (sometimes spelled Kenaniah), mentioned in verse 22, who was in charge of the singing. The reason he was put in charge of the singing, according to this scripture, was because *"he was skillful at it."*

Chenaniah, who appears to have come from the Gershonites, was the choir director. He had the ability to teach the singers and make sure they were prepared to sing whenever King David summoned them. Bringing the Ark back to Jerusalem was only the first of many times David would call for the choir.

With the musicians and singers in place, 1 Chronicles 15:25 states that David, with all the commanders, leaders, musicians, and singers, brought the Ark from the house of Obed-Edom with rejoicing. Verses 27 and 28 further describe this joyous celebration:

> *Now David was clothed in a robe of fine linen, as were all the Levites who were carrying the ark, and as were the singers, and Kenaniah, who was in charge of the singing of the choirs. David also wore a linen ephod. So all Israel brought up the ark of the covenant of the LORD with shouts, with the sounding of rams' horns and trumpets, and of cymbals, and the playing of lyres and harps.*
>
> 1 Chronicles 15:27-28

After the Ark was returned to Jerusalem, it *"had rest"* (1 Chronicles 6:31, KJV). It was at this time that David appointed musicians and singers to minister before the Lord continually (see verse 32).

When this permanent resting place was provided by David during his reign, it was no longer necessary for the Levites to carry the Ark. Their duties were changed to include assisting priests, judges, and scribes, and being gatekeepers and musicians, which, of course, included singers.

David appointed musicians and singers for the sole purpose of ministering unto the Lord continually with songs of praise and thanksgiving. The Levites were the leaders in the area of singing praises to God.

They were the Israelite choir. David's only reason for establishing a music ministry was to provide a comfortable habitation for the presence of the Lord.

Today, the purpose for a music ministry has not changed. We are to minister to the Lord and sing praises to Him for His pleasure and for His glory, always being aware of His presence among us. We must never get away from this central focus.

David had such an impact on temple worship that succeeding kings modeled their worship after the order he had established. When Hezekiah became king, he stationed the temple musicians *"in the way prescribed by David"* (2 Chronicles 29:25). The young King Josiah also made sure temple worship took place as commanded by David (see 2 Chronicles 35:15). Nehemiah, some five hundred years after David's reign, made sure the music was ministered *"according to the commandment of David the man of God"* (Nehemiah 12:24, KJV). No wonder God described David as *"a man after his own heart"* (1 Samuel 13:14).

King David took great care and detail in making sure the praises of God went up continually before the Lord. No king before or after him could boast of such music ministry organization with the express purpose of giving glory to God. Even when David was old and ready to pass the kingly torch to his son Solomon, he made sure that proper temple worship would take place long after he was gone.

David gave specific instructions as to what the Levites' duties would be under Solomon's leadership. Out of the twenty-four thousand Levites set aside for the work of the temple, David designated four thousand to praise the Lord with musical instruments (see 1 Chronicles 23:1-5). Their express duties are further described in verses 30 through 32. These included singing before the Lord morning and night, as well as at special festivals and feasts:

> *They were also to stand every morning to thank and praise the LORD. They were to do the same in the evening and whenever burnt offerings were presented to the Lord on Sabbaths and at New Moon festivals and at appointed feasts. They were to serve before the LORD regularly in the proper number and in the way prescribed for them. And so the Levites carried out their responsibilities for the Tent of Meeting, for the Holy Place and, under their brothers the descendants of Aaron, for the service of the temple of the LORD.*
>
> 1 Chronicles 23:30-32

God is always looking for those with the Levite spirit. He wants those who are willing to repent of their mistakes and return to Him. Remember, the name Levi means "to be attached, to join or be joined to." God knew the Levites were not mistake-proof, but He also knew that whatever they did, they would always repent and rejoin themselves to Him and also with one another in temple worship. To be effective in the music ministry we must always be aware of the importance of adjoining or aligning ourselves with the Father and of joining or connecting ourselves with one another.

It is important to notice in the history of Israel that there was no congregation for whom the choir sang. There was never a congregation in the temple. The children of Israel would worship from the Outer Court. The only ones actually in the temple were the priests and the Levites, and they were ministering unto the Lord. The singing of the Levites was not for the benefit of the people; it was only for the pleasure of the Father.

Although the New Covenant opened the door for all to come into the temple and worship, the purpose for music and singing in the temple has not changed. The ministry of music must always be directed first to the Lord and be for His glory. The congregation receives the residual benefit of the singing, but the central theme and focus should always be to minister to the Lord, thus providing a habitation for His presence.

Review Questions for Chapter 1

1. Who did God originally choose for the music ministry and why?

   _____

2. What are some of the steps God took to separate these ministers?

   _____

3. What were some of the duties of the Levites, and how were they paid?

   _____

4. Who in the Bible was most noted for their organization of the music ministry?

   _____

5. What do you remember most about this person regarding his work in the music ministry?

   _____

Points to Ponder for Chapter 1

1. How would I respond today to Moses' ageless question: "Who is on the Lord's side"?

_____

2. Could I consider myself one of God's "gifts" to the Body of Christ?

_____

3. Have I, like the Levites, recognized all of my mistakes and returned to the Lord?

_____

4. Does my music minister healing and deliverance, as God intended?

_____

5. Have I proven myself worthy of carrying the Ark, the presence of the Lord?

_____

Chapter 2

Requirements for Ministering in the Temple

—◆—

There were in biblical times, and still are today, certain requirements that must be met before a person can minister in the temple of the Lord. Simply having the ability to sing or play an instrument is only a fraction of what it takes to be an effective music minister. Remember, anybody can praise (Judah), but it takes those with the spirit of Levi to be effective in ministry.

God took the Levites through a process of preparation before they ever sang a note. They had to meet His requirements before He would allow them to be His special praise force. Likewise, before we can minister, we must also meet His requirements. In taking another brief look at the calling of the Levites, we see that there are five requirements which must be met before we can effectively serve. They are:

1. Make a Decision
2. Kill What's Dear to You
3. Be Thoroughly Cleansed
4. Carry the Burden
5. Have the Ability to Minister

Make a Decision

When Moses asked the question, *"Who is on the Lord's side?"*, the Levites were the only tribe to decide to gather themselves where Moses was, thus choosing to be on the Lord's side. This is the first step to meeting God's requirements for ministry. The decision the Levites made was a life decision to follow God and all His ways.

This was not a decision to be involved in ministry. Their decision had nothing to do with working in the temple or singing in a choir. It was a decision to turn from their wicked ways and follow the Lord.

Likewise, our decision to be on the Lord's side should have nothing to do with any aspirations we may have to minister. The decision we make to surrender our lives to God is based solely on the fact that we have recognized the error of our ways and realize that He is the only one who can bring about a true change in us.

We cannot consider our salvation as a stepping stone, or a means, to an end. Our decision to live for Christ is the single most important decision we will ever make.

With all the talent you may possess, would you still love God and wholly dedicate your life to Him if He told you never to sing or play an instrument again? Would this change your life decision? When we make a decision to be on the Lord's side, we embark on a new and exciting road toward fulfilling God's will for our lives.

A portion of His will for our lives might entail being involved in the music ministry. But the overall ramifications of our decision extend far beyond what we feel called to do.

The Levites made their decision because they wanted to save their lives. They never expected God to call them to the full-time ministry. They were just glad to escape His wrath. They were just glad to be saved.

It really is no different with us. At least it shouldn't be. Our decision to come to Christ should be because we realize that He's the only one who can save us from sin and death. This should be the only motivation for our decision.

After we make this decision, then we should earnestly seek His guidance as to how we can best serve Him. If God calls us to the music ministry, great. But if He doesn't, that's okay too. We're still saved and have escaped the inevitable wrath that is to come. That's the most important thing!

Kill What's Dear to You

When the Levites decided to go to where Moses was, they were also making the decision to forsake the ways of the other eleven tribes. They actually left their family and friends to join with Moses. This had to be a hard thing for them to do. But what was even harder was what they were instructed to do next:

> Then he said to them, "This is what the LORD, the God of Israel, says: 'Each man strap a sword to his side. Go back and forth through the camp from one end to the other, each killing his brother and friend and neighbor.' " The Levites did as Moses commanded, and that day about three thousand of the people died.
>
> Exodus 32:27-28

The Levites were commanded to kill their own brothers, sisters, friends, and neighbors. They had spent countless days with their fellow tribesmen, especially during their captivity in Egypt. They had experienced the joy of leaving Egypt together and the miracle of crossing the Red Sea on dry ground. But this was God's way of cleansing the entire camp of evil.

For the Levites, family, friends, and neighbors were near and dear, but they also represented idolatry against God. Anything or anyone who becomes a god to us, other than the true and living God, must be destroyed. Idolatry is an abomination to God, whether it involves people or things. Nothing should ever stand in the way of our relationship with God or the call He has placed on our lives.

Now, that doesn't mean that we should literally go out and kill someone today. God's grace for us today simply requires that we separate ourselves from these hindrances and cut off any evil associations.

What are those things that could be considered idols in our lives? God is asking us to search the camp of our heart, mind, and soul and kill whatever could ultimately cause us to be separated from Him. Paul encouraged us to mortify, or put to death, the deeds of the flesh (see Colossians 3:5-10). This is not an easy thing to do, and I'm sure it wasn't easy for the Levites. But, as with the Levites, God wants to make sure that there is no evil in our camp. We have to be willing to destroy those things that are holding us back. If we kill these things, then we have moved one step closer to qualifying for ministry unto the Lord.

Be Thoroughly Cleansed

Before the Levites could do any work in the temple they had to be cleansed:

29

The Lord said to Moses: "Take the Levites from among the other Israelites and make them ceremonially clean. To purify them, do this: Sprinkle the water of cleansing on them; then have them shave their whole bodies and wash their clothes, and so purify themselves."

Numbers 8:5-7

First, the sprinkling of the water signified that an impurity had been recognized and cleansed. This is symbolic of water baptism, which is the acceptance, recognition, and submission of man's sinful nature to God for cleansing.

Water is also symbolic of the Holy Spirit. After we have made the initial decision to follow Christ, the Holy Spirit comes to finish the work, cleansing us from dead works. This is our spiritual coronation. We are officially set aside, thoroughly washed, and anointed for service.

The purification process which the Levites went through did not just happen once. They were purified each time they were to enter the temple for service (see Exodus 40:32). Likewise, the purification process the Holy Spirit takes us through is continual. It doesn't just happen once. We need to be spiritually cleansed each time we are to minister in a service.

The shaving of the body hair was another outward sign of separation from the world. It symbolized total submission to God by laying aside every weight and *"sin which doth so easily beset us"* (Hebrews 12:1, KJV). We often become dusty, or dirty, from being in this world, even though we're not of this world. The Holy Spirit teaches us how to wash and shave in order to be ready for temple service. It is up to us to submit daily to this cleansing process.

> *Therefore, brothers, since we have confidence to enter the Most Holy Place by the blood of Jesus, by a new and living way opened for us through the curtain, that is, his body, and since we have a great priest over the house of God, let us draw near to God with a sincere heart in full assurance of faith, having our hearts sprinkled to cleanse us from a guilty conscience and having our bodies washed with pure water.*
>
> Hebrews 10:19-22

There are two major areas in our lives which require continual purification. First, those things we think on, or ponder, in our heart, and secondly, the things we actually do. Unless these areas are purified, we cannot enter into the service of the temple.

David asked a very important question as it related to his personal desire to be accepted into God's presence:

Who shall ascend into the hill of the LORD? or who shall stand in his holy place?

Psalm 24:3, KJV

31

David wanted to know who could actually be where God dwelt. Who can stand or serve in the house of the Lord? As it relates to us, what type of person is fit to minister in the holy place? David records the answer in the next verse:

> *He that hath clean hands, and a pure heart; who hath not lifted up his soul unto vanity, nor sworn deceitfully.*
>
> Psalm 24:4, KJV

God gave David four different answers to his one question. The first two are to have clean hands and a pure heart. This represents both our deeds and the motives behind our deeds. In other words, what we do and why we do it. Our deeds can be no purer than the motives behind them.

Are there hidden reasons for you wanting to render service in the temple? Our motives will determine whether we're accepted in the holy place.

The third requirement speaks of any idols we may have hidden away in our lives. Again, idols represent people or things we value more than our relationship with God. We can never enter into the most holy place if there are other idols we're bowing to.

The fourth requirement is the truthfulness of the vow we have made to God, which is closely related to our motives. Our vow to God can never be any more genuine than our motives. Our vow also cannot be genuine if we have not removed all of the idols from our lives.

God's reply to David was simple. Let everything you do and think be clean and pure. Make sure there are no idols in your life. Be truthful and unwavering in your vow to Him.

This idea of purification is not a state of being, but rather a process of becoming. Our motives and deeds are continually being purified for service. God has already provided grace for our many blunders and mistakes. Although we're not perfect, the key is to always strive for "purefection" in Him. Be willing to submit to the Holy Spirit's many washings and shavings during this process.

Carry the Burden

After the Levites were ceremonially cleansed, there were specific duties they were required to fulfill before they could sing or serve in any ministerial capacity:

> *After you have purified the Levites and presented them as a wave offering, they are to come to do their work at the Tent of Meeting.*
>
> Numbers 8:15

Before the Levites were able to minister in the temple, they had to set up the tent and properly arrange the furniture. They had to carry in all the temple articles, making sure everything was properly placed.

The fourth chapter of Numbers describes the Levites' duties of carrying the temple articles. The three families, which were from the three sons of Levi, each had something different to carry:

At the LORD's command through Moses, each was assigned his work and told what to carry.

Numbers 4:49

This fourth chapter begins by describing what the Kohathites had to carry. They were responsible for carrying the most holy things (see verse 4). This included the Ark of Testimony, the Lamp Stand, the Table of Shewbread, and all the holy furnishings and articles within the temple and Most Holy Place. They would never actually touch the temple articles, but, instead, were instructed to wrap them in blue cloth, cover them with badgers' skins, and put them in a special carrying frame (see verse 12).

The Gershonites were responsible for carrying the curtains of the tabernacle and the Tent of Meeting (see verses 25-26). They were instructed to wrap the curtains in the same manner as the Kohathites.

The Merarites were responsible for carrying the frames, crossbars, posts, and anything else that pertained to the infrastructure of the tabernacle (see verses 31-32). They would also wrap everything in the prescribed manner.

The carrying of these temple articles by the Levites is symbolic of them having a burden for the ministry. In the same manner, before we can minister in the temple, we must have a burden for the area to which we're called. We can learn much from what each Levitical family had to carry.

The temple articles and furnishings the Kohathites carried represented the presence and anointing of God. Like the Kohathites, we should have a burden to see the presence and anointing of God manifested in our services for healing and deliverance.

The name for the curtains which the Gershonites carried comes from the Hebrew word *yara,* meaning "to be broken, or grievous." [3] As with the Gershonites, we should be grieved over hurting members in the congregation who need a touch from God.

The name for the pillars the Merarites carried comes from the Hebrew word *amad*, which means "to appoint, to ordain or to confirm." [4] Like the Merarites, we should have a burden for the general infrastructure, or framework, of the church where we have been called and appointed to minister. Our call to minister cannot be separate from the vision of our local church and leadership.

Having a genuine burden for the ministry will always result in one thing: the desire to pray. This is the only way we can truly shoulder the burden we have for the ministry. In the same manner in which the Levites wrapped the temple articles in blue cloth and then badgers' skins, the burden we carry must first be wrapped and tied in prayer and then covered by the Spirit of God.

Anything carried in or by our flesh will be contaminated. It is rendered useless in the temple, and unacceptable to the Father. The burden we have for the ministry can only be carried in cloths made of effectual fervent prayers.

Have the Ability to Minister

God will never call us to something that He knows we don't have the ability to carry out. Not everyone can play an instrument. Not everyone can sing. If God has called you to the specific ministry of music, and you have a call and burden for that ministry, then no doubt you have been given the ability to perform the duties of that call.

The Bible says that Chenaniah was put in charge of the singing *"because he was skillful at it"* (1 Chronicles 15:22). All of the musicians and singers whom David chose were skillful enough to minister in song.

Along with their relatives—all of them trained and skilled in music for the LORD—they numbered 288.

1 Chronicles 25:7

It should always be our desire to give God our best. For this reason, auditioning of singers and musicians is always in order. The purpose of an audition is not to weed out bad singers, or even to identify good singers. There will always be some who are more talented than others. The real purpose of an audition is to see if an individual has any potential in the area of music.

There are a lot of people who are called to sing, but they just don't know it yet. Maybe, for some reason, they were discouraged from singing at a young age, or they just don't sing enough to realize how much potential they possess.

When I audition singers I don't listen for perfection; I listen for potential. When I hear someone sing, and they have potential, this lets me know God has invested a musical gift in them. As minister of music, it's my job to draw that gift out of them so that it can be nurtured to its fullest potential.

What do you do with a person who doesn't seem to have an ear for music? This is a hard question to answer, because you don't want to discourage anyone from praising God. Just as it's up to me to draw out the musical gift of someone who has potential, it's also my responsibility to redirect a person who doesn't have that potential in the hope that they will discover their true call. Again, we must give God our best. When He appoints, He equips and anoints.

There have been occasions when I've tried to help a person discover their true call because they clearly did not have an ear for music. I sometimes have instructed them to work on something vocally and then invited them to audition again at a later date. If, after the second audition, there was still no display of potential, I let them know that, in my opinion, their call was probably not to the music ministry.

You always want to be honest with people. If you allow someone into the choir who is unable to match tones (sing the exact notes you play on a piano), you make it difficult for others. In a sense, you're actually allowing that person to be misguided in his or her pursuit to fulfill the correct call on their life.

Once these five basic requirements are met, we can be assured of godly success in our temple ministry endeavors. Have you met all of His requirements?

Review Questions for Chapter 2

1. Name the five requirements that must be met before we can effectively serve in music ministry:

   a._____

   b._____

   c._____

   d._____

   e._____

Points to Ponder for Chapter 2

1. Have I made my decision to enter the music ministry with pure motives?

   _____

2. Is there something displeasing to the Lord in me that must die before I can bless others?

   _____

3. Have I been thoroughly washed and cleansed, even from recent bad thoughts and actions, and anointed for service?

   _____

4. Do I have a genuine burden to carry my share of the spiritual load?

   _____

5. Am I specifically called to music ministry?

   _____

Chapter 3

And Now, a Selection From the Choir

In most churches today, both large and small, the major thrust of the music program is the church choir. The choir ministry plays a major role in assuring that the congregation is edified and uplifted during services. For this reason, it is important that every choir member understand their purpose.

The central focus and vision for a choir ministry can easily be blurred into an ineffective time of entertainment, if its underlying purpose is anything different than what God originally designed. Myles Munroe says, "When you don't know the purpose of a thing, abuse is imminent." Many choirs are suffering from abuse because they've been abnormally used. And they're ineffective because they haven't understood their purpose as a choir ministry. One way to discover this purpose is to study just what having a choir is all about.

What does the word *choir* really mean? It can be defined as "a body of trained singers or that part of a church occupied by them; any band or organized company of dancers or singers." [5] According to this standard definition, a choir is a body, a band, or an organized company of trained singers. It is a group of people working together toward the same goal. This definition denotes oneness, unity, and togetherness.

The word *band*, as used in this definition, further emphasizes this togetherness. It is defined as "a company of persons associated, organized, or bound together." [6]

A choir has a common thread of association, one point of identification that solidifies the members as a distinguished, or set-aside, group. They are joined together for one purpose. If this togetherness or unity is not present, by definition, what they have is not a choir.

Possessing the attributes of this definition, however, is merely the beginning. The dictionary only describes the physical characteristics of a choir. We must also look at the spiritual characteristics of the choir, for it is in the Spirit that there is life and liberty. If a choir has no spiritual meaning or significance, there is only dead togetherness.

or tone, which comes out of the mouth. This simple process provides us with a common theme that will be evident in each definition of *singers* we discuss.

Look once again at the process of singing, and notice the key action words and phrases: "moves up," "passes over," "vibration," and "comes out." All of these words denote some type of movement.

Singing is an action word, and there's always some type of movement associated with music. The above process describes physical movement, but there is also movement that takes place in the Spirit when a choir begins to sing.

Have you ever heard someone say, "That was a very moving song"? This means that there was something about the song and those who sang it that caused a reaction in the listeners' emotions and spirit. It touched their heartstrings. The movement, or vibration, of a song causes a reaction in the innermost parts of our being. Music, by voice or instrument, has the ability to tap into the Spirit realm and command change.

Each time David played his harp for King Saul, who was vexed by an evil spirit, something happened:

Saul was refreshed, and was well, and the evil spirit departed from him.

1 Samuel 16:23, KJV

44

And Now, a Selection From the Choir

When a song is ministered in the right spirit (and we know that David was a man after God's own heart), it brings about positive change. It causes principalities to move. Just like the movement of physical air causes a vibration of sound, the movement of the Spirit, in music, causes a vibration of change. As singers, we must not only be aware of this movement; we must also be ready to move with the Spirit.

"Strolling like a minstrel" expresses this idea of movement even more clearly. It means "to sing as you go, or go as you sing." During Medieval times a minstrel would travel from town to town singing to the accompaniment of a harp or flute. The minstrel was able to affect more people through singing, if he or she moved while singing. As a matter of fact, 1 Samuel 18:6 is used to explain the root of this definition:

> And it came to pass as they came, when David was returned from the slaughter of the Philistine, that the women came out of all cities of Israel, singing and dancing, to meet king Saul, with tabrets, with joy, and with instruments of music.
>
> 1 Samuel 18:6, KJV

These women strolled as they sang. They came from their various towns, singing and dancing together with musical instruments. In this case, the movement was more for celebration.

45

But this is not the only type of movement described in the definition of *shuwr*. It can also be mournful, defensive, or offensive. This means that when we sing, we should be aware of the occasion and adjust, or move toward, that purpose. A choir must be aware of what's taking place in the spiritual realm while they're singing and be ready to move, if necessary.

To Turn or Travel About

This definition sheds further light on the unique characteristics and function of a choir from a spiritual perspective. Here, singers are likened to both a harlot and a merchant, who each, for different reasons, are always on the go, turning and traveling from place to place. Usually, when a person turns, he's turning his attention from one thing to another. At one point in time, he was focused on one thing, but then something else catches his eye. This causes him to turn and travel toward whatever it is that has gotten his attention.

A harlot or prostitute is always on the go, constantly turning from one paying customer to another. A merchant or traveling salesman is also going from place to place, turning here and there, in an attempt to sell his goods. But how does this relate to a choir? What causes the singers to turn and travel about? Where are they going?

Going Around for Inspection

The idea of movement is evident in this definition as well. Singers are to move around a particular area with the intent to inspect. An armed guard makes rounds on his watch. He never stays in one place. He has an area that he must guard and inspect to make sure that there are no hidden dangers or unwanted intruders. If there are, he must turn and move toward them with the intent of removing them from the premises.

As we look closer at this particular Hebrew definition, we find that it more specifically means "to spy out, to survey, to lurk for evil, to care for good, to lay wait, to observe, to perceive, and to see." [8] It is the choir's responsibility to go around for inspection. This is done by taking a spiritual survey of the area they're assigned to protect. They are to be on watch for evil, while at the same time caring for the good. Singers are to be spiritually alert and on guard, discerning the spiritual environment around them.

I'm reminded of Jesus' instructions to His disciples in the garden of Gethsemane. He told them:

Watch and pray.

Matthew 26:41

Jesus could feel the demons of death hovering over Him like vultures. He knew that it was just a matter of time before He would have to temporarily surrender to them. He was overwhelmed and sorrowful almost to the point of death. He could sense death all around Him.

Even at this most desperate time in His earthly life, Jesus wanted to teach His disciples one last lesson. He wanted them to be aware of the evil around them. He told them to be on watch, not so much for His sake, but for theirs.

Peter never forgot this very serious episode with Jesus, and even hints of its effects on his life when he later wrote:

> Be self-controlled and alert. Your enemy the devil prowls around like a roaring lion looking for someone to devour. Resist him, standing firm in the faith, because you know that your brothers throughout the world are undergoing the same kind of sufferings.
>
> 1 Peter 5:8-9

It is every choir member's responsibility to be spiritually alert in order to present a defense against the attacks and sabotage of the enemy.

Peter states two things in the above verses. First, be sober enough to identify the devil and his tricks. Second, once you have identified the evil, resist it. James also stated:

> Resist the devil, and he will flee from you.
>
> James 4:7

I used to think this idea of resisting the devil simply meant to reject or turn away from what he was offering. For example, when a salesman comes to your door, you can say, "No, thank you, I'm not interested," and then you close the door. This may work on a salesman, but not on the devil.

The word *resist* in the New Testament means "to stand against, oppose, or withstand." [9] It is taken from the Greek root word *anti,* which means "opposite."

Most of us have had an opposing view on something, an anti-crime bill, for example. We should all be opposed to the devil, or anti-devil. When the devil comes to our door, we can't just say, "No, thank you," and close the door. We must violently remove him from our property and our neighborhood as well.

In the same manner, a choir must firmly stand in opposition against whatever the devil may try to "sell" to God's people, violently opposing him until he flees. They must resist the devil in order to ensure the good is cared for and protected. The "good" is the Word of God and His people.

The congregation is under attack during a church service because the devil doesn't want the Word of God to fall on good ground. The devil is therefore constantly trying to see who he can distract, defeat, and ultimately destroy. It is the choir's responsibility, through their ministry in song, to care for the congregation by getting rid of all the distractions. This ultimately clears the path for complete deliverance in the service.

When a choir stands to sing in a service, many things are set in motion in the Spirit realm. Any evil spirits present immediately recognize that they're about to be assaulted. They'll try to distract the listener by tightening the grips of oppression and depression. Demons know the power of anointed music, for they experienced it in heaven. Their leader, Satan, was originally created to bring forth music to the glory of God.

Demons know that if the listener receives the Word of Truth through music, they'll be set free, and every demon will have to flee. The demon does all he can to make sure the listener cannot receive his or her deliverance. When a choir begins to sing, therefore, it's this battle they must "turn" their spiritual attention to. Any evil present must be uprooted by the choir.

The choir, in the Spirit, is searching out their territory, which is the congregation. Any evil is considered an unwanted intruder and must be expelled.

The singers must collectively go around for inspection and be ready to go to battle against the enemy:

For we wrestle not against flesh and blood, but against principalities, against powers, against

*the rulers of the darkness of this world, against
spiritual wickedness in high places.*

Ephesians 6:12, KJV

The fact is that we do wrestle. It's not against people, but against evil forces which we cannot see with our physical eyes. It's a spiritual battle.

Each individual choir member must sing with this purpose in mind, that they're sending forth deliverance to God's people. As they sing praises to the Lord, He's setting ambushes which are targeted for those principalities which have dared to trespass on holy ground. The choir is singing boldly, with strength and authority, realizing that the power of God is setting captives free.

Paul went on to describe how we are to fight against the devil by putting on the whole armor of God (see Ephesians 6:13-18). The choir is an army that must be well prepared in order to defeat its enemy. There can be no breaking of ranks, no insubordination, and no soldiers going spiritually AWOL. This army must fight as one. The deliverance of God's people depends on it. An unprepared army, or an army that doesn't know why it's fighting, is assured of defeat.

Paul said one last thing right after he described the armor, something that further emphasizes the importance of a choir's duty to inspect its territory. He instructed the Church to watch with infinite endurance for all saints:

Be alert and always keep on praying for all the saints.

Ephesians 6:18

We must remember that an army is necessary for the protection of the people, not just for ourselves. Therefore, when a choir sings, they're going out on the front line of the Spirit realm, representing the congregation. They must watch and be alert lest the enemy ambush God's people.

A Wall

The fourth definition, or characteristic, of a choir is a wall. In general, a wall encloses or encircles that which it desires to protect. It separates one thing from another, usually for the purpose of protection. The choir ministry serves as a wall of protection from evil on behalf of the good. They shield the congregation from any evil forces.

This wall is built so high that nothing can get over it, it's so deeply rooted in the Spirit that nothing can go under it, and so thick with the anointing that nothing can go through it. A choir should be so tightly knit spiritually that nothing can penetrate its wall of defense.

And Now, a Selection From the Choir

The enemy will definitely try to get through it. That's why it's so important that there be no holes, or gaps, in the wall. The choir ministry must be united and spiritually consistent so that nothing can permeate its wall.

Every choir member must have the same vision, and they must all speak and sing as one united force. The devil and his demons will constantly scale the wall trying to find the slightest opening. They will try to push against it to see how strong it is. A choir must withstand the pressure and adversity in order to gain a spiritual victory. The united members must form a spiritual fortress that cannot be infiltrated.

If the devil can get in by causing division, he will. If he can knock a hole in the wall with gossip, he will. He'll stop at nothing to break through that wall of protection.

A great example of a choir demonstrating the characteristics of a wall is found in 2 Chronicles 20. This chapter begins with a vast army making war against King Jehoshaphat. The king prayed and then received a word from the Lord through Jahaziel:

Do not be afraid or discouraged because of this vast army. For the battle is not yours, but God's. Tomorrow march down against them.

2 Chronicles 20:15-16

I love this last statement, because it shows that God wants a choir that is spiritually aggressive toward the

53

enemy. That's easy to do, once you've realized that the battle is not yours, but God's. He just wants you to be in the right place at the right time, and to do exactly what He says, when He says. Then, and only then, is victory inevitable.

Following this prophecy, Jehoshaphat and all of Israel had a church service. The Levites led the praise and worship. This put Israel in the right frame of mind and spirit to march against their enemies. The next morning they set out toward the enemy camp.

Notice what King Jehoshaphat's instructions were. He appointed singers to sing as they marched toward the enemy. Remember, a choir must be ready to move. In this case, the singers went out ahead of the army.

> *After consulting the people, Jehoshaphat appointed men to sing to the LORD and to praise him for the splendor of his holiness as they went out at the head of the army, saying:* **"Give thanks to the LORD, for his love endures forever."**
>
> 2 Chronicles 20:21

The choir marched as a wall of protection for those who carried the weapons. It was the choir that ensured safe passage for those with swords, not the other way around.

And Now, a Selection From the Choir

The Sword of the Spirit is the Word of God (see Ephesians 6:17), and the pastor is the one who delivers this Word. It is, therefore, the choir's responsibility to go before the pastor with anointed and powerful praise to the Lord, in order to clear the way for the Word to fall on good ground.

The members of the choir must march forward spiritually advancing toward the enemy. As with King Jehoshaphat, the result will always be complete and decisive victory!

> *As they began to sing and praise, the LORD set ambushes against the men of Ammon and Moab and Mount Seir who were invading Judah, and they were defeated.*
>
> 2 Chronicles 20:22

As the praises go forth, God is the One who actually fights the battle. The choir's only responsibility is to be united as one, a wall-like fortress advancing toward the enemy. When the choir does this, there is no place for the devil to go but out!

Paul stated:

> *Neither give place to the devil.*
>
> Ephesians 4:27, KJV

The Greek word translated as *"place"* is *topos,* which means "a spot, a location, an opportunity, or license." [10] The word *topos* is where we get our

English word *topography*. *Topography* is "a description of the physical features of a region. It describes the various physical characteristics of an entire neighborhood." [11] I believe that what Paul was saying was this: "Don't even allow the devil into your neighborhood." As a collective body of singers, a choir cannot allow the devil into their spiritual territory.

Paul knew that the devil was very territorial, and he still is! He'll try to take advantage of every little space we leave open. This is why it's important for the choir to understand its purpose and role as a collective body advancing toward the enemy. The choir is to be an anointed musical fortress, clearing the path for the deliverance of God's people.

Review Questions for Chapter 3

1. What are the four basic meanings of the word "singers"?

   a._____

   b._____

   c._____

   d._____

2. To whom did the first choirs in the Bible sing?

_____

Points to Ponder for Chapter 3

1. Do I understand God's original purpose for the choir ministry?

   _____

2. Does my music move people?

   _____

3. Am I willing to serve as a guard over God's flock, to prevent evil from approaching and to deal with it when it does appear?

   _____

4. Have I put on "the whole armor of God"?

   _____

5. Am I spiritually strong enough to serve as a wall of protection for others?

   _____

The Choir's Attire

What should a choir wear when they minister in the house of the Lord? Should each choir member wear the same thing? The choirs during King David's time did.

> *Now David was clothed in a robe of fine linen,*
> *as were all the Levites who were carrying the*
> *ark, and as were the singers, and Kenaniah,*
> *who was in charge of the singing of the choirs.*
>
> 1 Chronicles 15:27

The entire choir wore the same thing, which happened to be a type of garment made of white linen. This must have looked very beautiful. White is symbolic of purity and integrity.

I'm in no way suggesting that all choirs wear white. I'm not even suggesting that a choir always wear the same colored garment. As a matter of fact, it really doesn't matter what the choir wears externally:

Man looks at the outward appearance, but the LORD *looks at the heart.*

1 Samuel 16:7

The outward adorning of a choir is only significant to the extent that it reflects the inward adorning. It's not important what a choir wears on the outside, if they're not wearing the same thing on the inside.

What should a choir wear when they minister in the house of the Lord? Should each choir member wear the same thing? If we're talking about inward adornment, then the answer is "Absolutely! Positively! Yes!"

We've already seen the choir as a spiritual army. With this in mind, let's look at the proper armor for a soldier in order to gain some insight as to what the attire of a choir should be. In his letter to the Ephesians, Paul mentioned six pieces of armor which help to both protect the soldier and attack the enemy.

In relating this armor to a choir, I believe that the most important piece of armor is *"the belt of truth"* (Ephesians 6:14). This belt is what holds the other pieces of armor in place. It keeps everything together and secure.

Any choir that desires to be effective must put on truth as their attire. Truth is the only thing that can hold a choir together. And not just any kind of truth, but the real Truth. Jesus said:

I am the way, the truth, and the life.

John 14:6, KJV

Jesus is the truth. Every aspect of His person, His every characteristic is founded upon truth. A choir must operate in this truth if it is to be effective in ministry. When a choir fails to operate in truth, their worship is fruitless, and their power is negated. As Jesus said:

But the hour cometh, and now is, when the true worshippers shall worship the Father in spirit and in truth: for the Father seeketh such to worship him. God is a Spirit: and they that worship him must worship him in spirit and in truth.

John 4:23-24, KJV

We, as believers, have seemingly mastered the art of worshiping God in spirit, while at the same time ignoring the importance of dealing in truth. Our worship is incomplete without this main ingredient.

The word *truth*, or *true*, is defined as "something that is not concealed, accurate, verified, certified, correct, valid, loyal, reliable, sincere, genuine, authentic, pure and real." [12] All of these are characteristics that each choir member must exhibit toward one another in order to operate in truth. Where there is truth, division cannot reside, for division cannot manifest itself in truth.

When a choir fails to operate in truth, division will always be present. As a result, their worship is without integrity. Instead of being accurate, it misses the spiritual target. Instead of being certified, it has no seal of God's approval. Instead of being pure, it's tainted. When a choir operates in this false realm, the congregation is simply being entertained, and the ultimate objective is never reached.

When a choir operates in truth, the congregation identifies with that truth, which leads to their deliverance. Jesus said:

And ye shall know the truth, and the truth shall make you free.

John 8:32, KJV

This is the truth we experience as a result of our knowledge of, and relationship with, Jesus Christ.

The truth of God must be in operation between our fellow brothers and sisters if our collective praise is to be effective. In Psalm 15, David asked the Lord an interesting question. We, as singers, must ask ourselves this same question if we're to wear the same attire:

The Choir's Attire

LORD, who shall abide in thy tabernacle? **Who shall dwell in thy holy hill?**

Psalm 15:1, KJV

As ministers in music, it should be our desire for the praises we offer to God to ascend to the holy hill of the Lord. What must we do to ensure that the Lord receives our praise? What must we do to ensure our place in the tabernacle of the Lord?

He that walketh uprightly, and worketh righteousness, and speaketh the truth in his heart.

Psalm 15:2, KJV

Our Christian walk and works of righteousness will always affect those around us. When our relationship with the Father is healthy and in focus, our relationships with one another will also tend to be healthy. This ultimately leads to truthful communication.

When we speak, we are directly communicating and interacting with another person. We cannot speak, or converse, with someone without having a direct effect on their life. Our spoken words will have either a positive or negative effect on those who hear them. Solomon wrote:

Death and life are in the power of the tongue: and they that love it shall eat the fruit thereof.

Proverbs 18:21, KJV

The writer James devotes an entire chapter to the power and dangers of the tongue. Read the third chapter of James to capture the full scope of his message. Allow me to briefly summarize the chapter here.

In the first few verses, James compares the tongue to the small bit that is placed into a horse's mouth, and also to the helm of a large ship. Both of these small things determine the direction something much larger will take. The bit determines the direction the horse will take, and the helm determines the direction a ship will take.

James goes on to say (in verse 6) that the tongue is a fire and has the power to burn up, or defile, the whole body. In other words, one unbridled tongue has the potential to go through and destroy an entire choir, much like a wildfire burns a forest.

James then says that although man has been able to tame all kinds of beasts, he has not yet been able to tame his own tongue, because it's so unruly and full of deadly poison (see verses 7-8). Another major concern of James' is the inherent hypocritical nature of the tongue, which is able to send forth both words of sweetness and curses of bitterness at the same time. James gives a quick, but powerful prelude to this third chapter in James 1:26:

The Choir's Attire

If anyone considers himself religious and yet does not keep a tight rein on his tongue, he deceives himself and his religion is worthless.

Everything we seek to accomplish in the choir ministry is utterly paralyzed if we cannot individually win the battle over the control of our tongue. I have seen many choirs destroyed because of seeds of destruction and division planted by a few of its members. If a choir is to ascend to that place David spoke of in Psalm 15, we must learn how to speak only the truth to one another.

We cannot repeat what we've heard from someone else. That's gossip, and it only helps to spread the wildfire. We can't speak based on speculation, because it's not confirmed truth and tends to plant seeds of doubt in the minds of those who hear it. We cannot even speak what we feel, unless it's under the unction of the Holy Spirit, because we're allowing our emotions to rule our tongue rather than the Spirit of God.

James, the obvious authority on the dangers of the tongue, encourages us:

Be swift to hear, slow to speak, slow to wrath.

James 1:19, KJV

As choir members, we must learn to speak only life and encouragement to one another. If we can do this, then and only then do we qualify to abide in the tabernacle of God's presence.

Returning to Psalm 15, David gave an additional answer to the question he posed in verse one:

He that backbiteth not with his tongue, nor doeth evil to his neighbour, nor taketh up a reproach against his neighbour.

Psalm 15:3, KJV

Your fellow choir member is your neighbor, and God is not pleased when we sing praises to Him, but cannot get along with or speak well of the person who's standing right next to us. We cannot minister truth as a choir, if we don't operate in truth on a regular basis. God desires *"truth in the inward parts"* (Psalm 51:6, KJV).

Review Questions for Chapter 4

1. What is more important than the outward attire of the choir?

   _____

2. Give a scripture reference for the answer to question 1.

   _____

3. What did I say I believed was the most important piece of armor a Christian soldier in music ministry could wear?

   _____

4. Give a scripture reference for your answer to question 3.

   _____

5. What happens when a choir fails to operate in truth?

   _____

Points to Ponder for Chapter 4

1. Is God pleased when He looks beyond my outward attire and sees my heart?

   _____

2. Can I truly say that I walk in truth?

   _____

3. Am I worthy to "abide" in the Lord's tabernacle?

   _____

4. Am I worthy to "dwell" on His "holy hill"?

   _____

5. Do I walk uprightly, work righteousness, and speak truth?

   _____

Chapter 5

Stop the Music!

—✦—

Have you ever been in a church service, and after the choir finished singing, you sensed that something just wasn't right? They sounded good vocally, but there was a distinct absence of God's anointing on their ministry. Your spirit man would not allow you to join in or to receive what was being presented.

You may have had some idea about what the problem could have been. Maybe you sensed that something was not right with the music director. Maybe the style of the song was not appropriate for church, and thus did not bring glory to the Lord. Maybe the choir was having some serious problems with division among its members and/or its leadership. Or it quite possibly could have been any combination of the above. One thing is for sure: any or all of the above situations can slowly drain God's anointing from a music ministry. If steps are not taken to deal with these issues, God's ultimate purpose for music ministry in the church will never be reached.

When music in a church is performed for the wrong reasons or by the wrong people, it ceases to be edifying. When this happens, adjustments should be made to ensure that the music in a service is spiritually edifying to all those who are listening. Until this happens, the music should stop!

This, of course, doesn't mean that you shut down the entire music department. It just means that you change or remove those elements which hinder the flow of God's anointing.

There are three basic reasons why the music ministry of a choir or band may need to be temporarily halted until the proper personnel or musical material can be found.

The Wrong Music Director

The music director is the one who's responsible for all the music within a church. He or she will usually decide what songs will be sung during an entire service, which includes praise and worship, special choir songs, solos, and instrumentals. The music director, for the most part, sets the spiritual atmosphere in the service. The choir and band will generally follow the music director's lead. Therefore the overall effectiveness of the music ministry is determined by the music director. If the music director has not truly submitted to the lordship of Christ and the leadership of the pastor, this can cause mass confusion and division within the choir and, ultimately, the congregation. This is exactly what took place in heaven.

When I was a little boy in church I used to hear preachers say that Satan was the choir director in heaven. This, of course, always got my attention, because I wanted to be a choir director. But I had a real problem with wanting to be like Satan. As I grew and began to study the validity of this statement, I realized that although there is no biblical evidence of him actually being a choir director, he was definitely heavily involved in the music of heaven.

There are very few descriptions of Satan, or Lucifer as he was then called, in the Bible. But the few we find give us some insight into what his responsibilities were during his time in heaven.

This name Lucifer actually appears only once in the Bible:

How art thou fallen from heaven, O Lucifer, son of the morning! how art thou cut down to the ground, which didst weaken the nations!

Isaiah 14:12, KJV

Literally, this passage describes the overthrow of a tyrant, the king of Babylon, but many Bible scholars see in this passage a description of Satan. He rebelled against the throne of God and was *"brought down to the grave, to the depths of the pit"* (Isaiah 14:15). [13] Notice in this chapter that Lucifer is described as having viols or harps (see verse 11). This gives some indication that he was specifically created by God for musical purposes.

His name, Lucifer, in its original Hebrew is the word *halal*. This is the same Hebrew word that is used to define praise. [14] It appears that Lucifer was the *halal* in heaven.

There is one other passage that seemingly describes many of Lucifer's characteristics. The prophet Ezekiel goes into great detail in describing this archangel named Lucifer. God created him, and anything that God creates is indescribably ornate and beautiful. There's absolutely no doubt in my mind that Lucifer was one of the most beautiful musical angels in all of heaven.

In looking at Ezekiel's description of him, we can see just how beautiful and musical he was:

This is what the Sovereign LORD says: "You were the model of perfection, full of wisdom and perfect in beauty. You were in Eden, the garden of God; every precious stone adorned you: ruby, topaz and emerald, chrysolite, onyx

*and jasper, sapphire, turquoise and beryl. Your
settings and mountings were made of gold; on
the day you were created they were prepared."*

Ezekiel 28:12-13

God created Lucifer so perfect that he was looked
upon by all the other angels as the model by which
they should be compared. Every precious stone you
could imagine was inset into his body.

These stones were set in and around gold *"tabrets
and pipes,"* which is how the King James Version of
the Bible renders this phrase, *"settings and mountings."* The tabret was a percussion instrument, much
like the modern-day tambourine. The use of the word
pipes, which is a type of wind instrument, suggests
that Lucifer had the ability to make sounds similar to
a trumpet, or possibly even a pipe organ. The viols
and harps mentioned in Isaiah 14:11 suggest that he
had musical strings attached to his body, and this
enabled him to sound like a violin, harp, or cello.

Take a moment and try to imagine the numerous
musical possibilities Lucifer possessed. He was a
walking, floating philharmonic orchestra. He was
uniquely created to give praise and glory to God.

*You were anointed as a guardian cherub, for so
I ordained you. You were on the holy mount of
God; you walked among the fiery stones.*

Ezekiel 28:14

Lucifer was in such close proximity to God's throne that when God breathed, His breath would blow through Lucifer's pipes and make the most beautiful music. The light of God would reflect off of Lucifer's many stones, creating a wonderful and breathtaking laser-light show. The other angels could hear and see Lucifer coming from afar, because of his indescribable music and reflective beauty. He was the major source of music in heaven.

Because of the way God created him, Lucifer couldn't walk without giving praise to God, he couldn't fly without giving praise to God, and he couldn't even breathe without praising God. Everything he did brought praise and glory to the One who created him, and he enjoyed it. Lucifer could quite possibly have been the minister of music in heaven, for he was held in very high esteem by his peers.

You were blameless in your ways from the day you were created till wickedness was found in you. Through your widespread trade you were filled with violence, and you sinned. So I drove you in disgrace from the mount of God, and I expelled you, O guardian cherub, from among the fiery stones. Your heart became proud on account of your beauty, and you corrupted your wisdom because of your splendor. So I threw you to the earth; I made a spectacle of you before kings.

Ezekiel 28:15-17

Stop the Music!

Jesus remembered that fateful day and gave His disciples a brief account of what happened:

I saw Satan fall like lightning from heaven.

Luke 10:18

Lucifer became lifted up in pride and began to look at his endless beauty and talents rather than on the One who had created him. Then, Lucifer's motives changed. Suddenly, he wanted to be like God and thus failed to submit himself to his ultimate authority.

As a result, God dismissed him, along with a host of angels whom Lucifer was able to influence. God not only relieved Lucifer of his duties; He also cast him out of heaven. Thus, God fired His main source of music and praise.

Think about it: for a period of time, heaven was without a minister of music. No longer could you hear the beautiful sounds of Lucifer on the mountain of God. No longer could you see his magnificent light presentations.

With all of the beauty, gifts, and talents that Lucifer possessed, he became useless to the Kingdom, and God had to stop his music. All heaven was affected, because the minister of music had the wrong spirit. So here is an important question for all pastors: if God Almighty can do without His main source of music in heaven for a season, can't you? There's never an appropriate time to put talents and gifts above character and integrity.

I've known cases in which a minister of music was a practicing homosexual. In others, I've seen music directors who, by their actions, made sure everyone knew that they were the star of the show. And I've often observed a music director's negative attitude and disrespect for his pastor, while at the same time he was operating a dictatorship over the choir. Needless to say, God is not pleased with this type of music director and will not place His blessing on any music that comes from this type of spirit. It's detrimental to the pastor, the music ministry, and the congregation.

We must follow the example of our heavenly Father, who would not settle for a minister of music who was simply gifted and talented. His standards of clean hands (representing our deeds) and a pure heart (representing our motives) must also be ours (see Psalm 24:4). If God can make changes and adjustments in His music program to ensure that His praise is pure, so can we.

It wasn't long after Lucifer's dismissal that God created man, that's us, to take the fallen one's place. He created us with hands to clap and raise in praise to Him. He gave us vocal chords (our strings) to sing His praises. He also made us *"lively stones,"* so that when the light of His presence shines on us, we can *"shew forth [His] praises"* (1 Peter 2:5 and 9, KJV). Now that's a light show! We are now and shall be forevermore God's chosen ministers of music. Praise God!

The Wrong Choir Member/s

It is the responsibility of the music director, with the help of the pastor, to ensure that people who want to be choir members have a real heart and desire to minister to the Lord. Prospective choir members who have wrong motives or unresolved personal issues need, first, to be ministered to before they can be effective in ministering to others. Allowing people with the wrong motives or the wrong spirit to enter the choir will weaken the overall effectiveness of the music ministry.

Choir members who have problems with jealousy, gossiping, low self-esteem, envy, and the like can cause division in the choir. A choir member who has difficulty submitting to leadership should not be allowed in the choir. God originally intended for the music ministry to be a sacred, pure, and holy ministry. It should remain as clean as He originally intended it to be. If it's not, we must stop the music until the proper adjustments can be made. This is exactly what Nehemiah did.

From the time of the Exodus of the children of Israel from Egypt, God set specific guidelines for them to follow to ensure that they would not be contaminated with evil from other nations. There were certain people and nations whom God expressly forbid them from dwelling with or marrying. He also forbid their enemies from joining with them in worship.

God knew that if He allowed this, it would eventually lead to the mixing of religious practices and, ultimately, idolatry. An example of this was God's order to stay clear of any Moabites or Ammonites:

> *No Ammonite or Moabite or any of his descendants may enter the assembly of the LORD, even down to the tenth generation. For they did not come to meet you with bread and water on your way when you came out of Egypt, and they hired Balaam son of Beor from Pethor in Aram Naharaim to pronounce a curse on you.*
>
> Deuteronomy 23:3-4

The Ammonites and Moabites were a long-standing enemy of the Lord's because they had not assisted Israel during their journey from Egypt. God did not want them to ever set foot in His assembly. They were not of the same kindred spirit as the children of Israel. The Ammonites and Moabites worshiped Baal. In addition, their origin was rooted in incest.

The birth of these tribes is recorded in the book of Genesis. They were direct descendants of Lot. After Lot and his two daughters fled from Sodom and Gomorrah, they settled in a cave in the mountains of Zoar. Lot's two daughters began to think that they would never be with a man in order to keep their family's bloodline alive, so, on two separate occasions, they made their father drunk and had intercourse with him:

Stop the Music!

So both of Lot's daughters became pregnant by their father. The older daughter had a son, and she named him Moab; he is the father of the Moabites of today. The younger daughter also had a son, and she named him Ben-Ammi; he is the father of the Ammonites of today.

Genesis 19:36-38

The ancestral bloodline of both the Moabites and Ammonites was rooted in sexual immorality, and it was this type of spirit that the Lord did not want in His most sacred assembly. This is very significant, because years later Nehemiah had to confront this same spirit.

Nehemiah was able to rally all Israel together to rebuild the wall of Jerusalem, and as they began the work, three archrivals came against them and tried to discourage them from rebuilding the wall. They were: Sanballat, Tobiah, and Geshem (see Nehemiah 2:19). There are many spiritual truths to be gained from the study of all three of these enemies, but of the three, Tobiah is probably mentioned more than the rest. He was the most outspoken.

It was Tobiah who outwardly mocked Nehemiah when he first mentioned rebuilding the wall (see Nehemiah 4:3), and Tobiah also sent letters to intimidate Nehemiah (see Nehemiah 6:19). Tobiah was an Ammonite, and he acted like one too.

Still, the wall of Jerusalem was built despite the efforts of Tobiah and his cohorts. When the construction was finished, Nehemiah organized a celebration service to dedicate it to the Lord. A description of this dedication service is given in Nehemiah 12:27-43.

The Levites were called and two choirs were assembled. The choirs, along with trumpeters and other musicians, sang and danced on top of the wall, and Nehemiah was right there with them. Then they took the celebration into the house of God (see Nehemiah 12:40). It was a joyous celebration, to say the least:

And on that day ... the women and children also rejoiced. The sound of rejoicing in Jerusalem could be heard far away.

Nehemiah 12:43

During the celebration someone began to read from the book of Moses:

On that day the Book of Moses was read aloud in the hearing of the people and there it was found written that no Ammonite or Moabite should ever be admitted into the assembly of God, because they had not met the Israelites with food and water but had hired Balaam to call a curse down on them.

Nehemiah 13:1-2

Thus, all of Israel was put in remembrance of God's decree to them years ago. When they heard this, they removed from the assembly all those of foreign descent. No doubt the one who read the Scriptures noticed some people who should not have been there. But there was one foreigner in the assembly that day that only a few knew about:

> *Before this, Eliashib the priest had been put in charge of the storerooms of the house of our God. He was closely associated with Tobiah, and he had provided him with a large room formerly used to store the grain offerings and incense and temple articles, and also the tithes of grain, new wine and oil prescribed for the Levites, singers and gatekeepers, as well as the contributions for the priests.*
>
> Nehemiah 13:4-5

Nehemiah's longtime enemy, Tobiah the Ammonite, was now actually living in the house of God. To make matters worse, Eliashib had allowed him to stay in the storeroom that held all the articles of worship, and they had been moved out in order to make room for Tobiah.

Included in these articles of worship was the oil, which represents the anointing. It would appear that the anointing was removed from the house of the Lord in order to make room for an idolatrous and rebellious spirit, one rooted in sexual immorality. The very room set aside for the worship of God was turned into a habitation for sexual immorality and rebellion against God.

The name Ammonite is taken from the Hebrew root *amam*, which means "to overshadow by huddling together." It also means "to become dim, or hide." [15] When you combine these two definitions, Ammonite literally means a hidden huddling together which overshadows and makes dim. This is a perfect description of a clique, which is simply a smaller group within a larger group, having a private agenda to tear down anyone outside of their little circle.

Cliques are divisive in nature. You can't always see them, but you know that they're there. They overshadow and cause the overall brightness of God's glory to be dimmed. This is one of the spirits which had taken up residence in the temple of the Lord.

When Nehemiah heard what had been taking place, he immediately stopped the celebration:

Here I learned about the evil thing Eliashib had done in providing Tobiah a room in the courts of the house of God. I was greatly displeased and threw all Tobiah's household goods out of the room. I gave orders to purify the rooms, and then I put back into them the equipment of the house of God, with the grain offerings and the incense.

Nehemiah 13:7-9

"The evil thing" that had been done made Nehemiah "sick to his stomach." The thought that articles of praise had actually been taken out of the house of God and had been replaced with all kinds of evil was too much for him to bear. He considered this an *"evil thing,"* because it was in total disobedience to God.

I love Nehemiah's response. He did three things many of us as pastors and music directors might need to do in our ministries. First, he threw out all of Tobiah's household goods. The King James Version of the Bible translates *"household goods"* as *"stuff."*

Secondly, Nehemiah ordered the room to be thoroughly cleansed and purified. He didn't want even the stench of evil in God's room.

Thirdly, he put the room back in order. The praise articles and the anointing were returned to the house of God.

Nehemiah had no tolerance for a wrong spirit in the house of God. He made those around him accountable to follow God's holy ordinances, in order to ensure that proper praise and worship would take place. And if you've allowed a spirit of Tobiah into your music department, you can do no less. Throw out the *"stuff,"* purify the rooms, and get back the anointing.

We cannot afford to allow anything to hinder the flow of God's Spirit. With all the great singing and praising that took place during Israel's celebration, God could not have been pleased, because there was no place or provision for His anointing. The Bible states that God inhabits, or is enthroned in, *"the praises of Israel [His people]"* (Psalm 22:3). But He cannot inhabit our praise if we have *"stuff"* in the storerooms of our heart.

The Wrong Music

It's very easy to slip into the all-too-familiar trap of trying to please man with our music, rather than God. Many times we choose songs for a service based on an expected response from the congregation. Our goal should be to select music that we feel will, first, bring glory to God and, second, bring edification to the congregation. When we select our material based solely on a response we expect from the people, we will begin to see a downward trend in our effectiveness. This is clearly because the words, or message, of our songs are directed more toward the people rather than God, when He is the only one who can deliver the people.

The musical accompaniment of our song is also, many times, geared toward a style to which we know the people will respond favorably. But when our music fails to meet the first criteria of bringing praise and glory to God, we must stop the music until changes in our repertoire can be made. We see an example of this in the book of First Samuel. The music should have been stopped, but, unfortunately, it wasn't. The end result was detrimental to all of Israel.

David had just killed Goliath. This was a feat that would have been considered a miracle—even if it had been accomplished by a grown man. David was just a young lad, probably about sixteen years of age. His conquering of Goliath was a surprise to everyone. Because of David's great triumph over Goliath, the entire Philistine army fled, and Israel was able to claim victory. This was cause for a celebration, and upon David's return from this great victory, some singing and dancing ensued.

When the men were returning home after David had killed the Philistine, the women came out from all the towns of Israel to meet King Saul with singing and dancing, with joyful songs and with tambourines and lutes.

1 Samuel 18:6

These women were jubilant and energetic in their singing and dancing. They came from near and far, from all the surrounding towns of Israel just to greet, with songs of praise, the mighty men of war. But there was something obviously wrong with their song selection:

As they danced, they sang: "Saul has slain his thousands, and David his tens of thousands."

1 Samuel 18:7

We know how the song made King Saul feel. He was very upset that the women would dare to compare him to a little boy (see verses 8-9). We don't really know how the song affected David. Here he was, a young boy thrust into a victory celebration as the hero.

But, more importantly, how did this celebration of song and dance make the Lord feel? Was it really King Saul or young David who deserved the praise? No! It was the Lord who caused David and all the Israelites to be victorious. So it was the Lord, and Him only, who should have been the central focus of the celebration. God was definitely not pleased with this song, because it didn't bring Him glory and it was not edifying to all of Israel. They were singing to the wrong king.

This is not at all surprising, since it was the people of Israel who asked God for a king in the first place. This had not been His original plan for their governance:

> But when they said, "Give us a king to lead us," this displeased Samuel; so he prayed to the LORD. And the LORD told him: "Listen to all that the people are saying to you; it is not you they have rejected, but they have rejected me as their king."
>
> 1 Samuel 8:6-7

The song the women now sang was an outward sign of the people's desire for an earthly king over their heavenly King. They were neglecting their true Source of victory, and someone should have stopped the music because it totally ignored the King of kings.

This one song and the failure to stop it had a rippling effect. King Saul became bitter toward David and spent the rest of his reign trying to hunt him down and kill him. Poor David spent the next fifteen or so years dodging spears, fleeing for his life, and living in and out of caves. And the children of Israel suffered because their king became insane. They also lost the benefit of a key leader in the person of David for many years.

Nothing good can ever come out of music that is geared specifically toward the praise and glory of man, rather than the Creator of man. Our song selection for church services must always, first, give total glory to God. We cannot sing songs that make people wonder who the song is talking about. God was not pleased with this in David's day, and He's still not pleased with it today.

Review Questions for Chapter 5

1. What are the three basic reasons that the music ministry of the church should sometimes be stopped?

   a. _____

   b. _____

   c. _____

2. Who appears to have been what we might call "heaven's choir leader"?

   _____

3. What was it that caused his downfall?

   _____

Points to Ponder for Chapter 5

1. Am I part of the problem in the church rather than the blessing God intended me to be?

   _____

2. Do I have any of the tendencies that caused Lucifer's downfall?

   _____

3. Am I misusing any of my musical gifts?

   _____

4. Am I fully submitted to God and to my church superiors?

   _____

5. Is the music I sing (or play) appropriate, that is, does it bring glory to God?

   _____

Chapter 6

Is There Really Strength in Numbers?

———✦———

There are many churches today, both large and small, that don't have a choir ministry as part of their music program. There are various reasons for this. Many pastors have opted, instead, for a smaller praise team of no more than about ten singers accompanied by a small band.

Although the definition of a choir does not specify a number, our assumption here, as is typically the case, is that a choir is much larger in number than a praise team. Some pastors simply have not found a qualified person to be choir director. Other pastors don't see a need for a choir ministry in their church. For them, the praise team fills all the music needs. This is due to the fact that the extent of their music is praise and worship, with a special solo here and there.

There are many pastors who would love to have a choir, but they just don't want the headaches commonly associated with bringing together so many different attitudes and personalities on a weekly basis. For some pastors, a choir is not in their plans at all. But for others, a choir ministry is something they definitely want in the future. Their current praise team is a step toward this goal.

If a church is to have a choir ministry, the pastor must first have a vision for and see a need for this ministry within his or her church. Not all pastors have this desire. But there are a few questions we need to ask ourselves. Can a praise team take the place of or accomplish the same things as a choir? Is the choir ministry necessary in light of the diversity and more simplistic makeup of the praise team? And finally, in comparing the choir ministry to the praise team ministry, is there really strength in numbers?

And the answers are: "No!" "Yes!" and "Yes!" No, a praise team cannot take the place of or accomplish the same things as a choir. Yes, the choir ministry is necessary in light of the diversity and more simplistic makeup of the praise team. And yes, in comparing the choir ministry to the praise team ministry, there is really strength in numbers.

I have nothing against the praise team ministry. I've worked with praise teams and smaller groups for most of my life. I personally enjoy the intimacy of these smaller groups. A praise team is a vital and useful tool for any church, especially for a mid-week service or prayer meeting where the attendance is smaller. But it can never take the place of the choir ministry, simply because the two are totally different in their function. This is due mainly to the difference in the number of people who are typically used in the choir, as opposed to the praise team.

God was always specific on matters concerning His temple, down to how many Levites should minister in song. David set aside four thousand to praise the Lord with musical instruments (see 1 Chronicles 23:5). This chapter later says of them:

They were to serve before the LORD regularly in the proper number and in the way prescribed for them.

1 Chronicles 23:31

Not all four thousand ministered at the same time. Rather, they ministered in shifts, so that music could be heard day and night.

A more reasonable number is found in 1 Chronicles 25:7:

They numbered 288.

Now, that was a choir! There's definitely strength in numbers, not so much for the physical makeup, but rather for the overall spiritual effect it has on the enemy.

The Lord is very clear on this matter. He knows that large groups of people, united for the single purpose of advancing His Kingdom, are intimidating to the devil. Do you remember what God did when the devil sent an army with horses and chariots to capture Elisha? Elisha's reply to his nervous servant was simple:

Those who are with us are more than those who are with them.

2 Kings 6:16

Remember, while we're giving praise to God, there are evil forces we're warring against in the spirit. The enemy doesn't want God to receive the praise, and he doesn't want the congregation to receive their deliverance, which often comes through the ministry of music. The number of singers we send out to battle will often determine the outcome.

When King Jehoshaphat appointed singers to go before his army, he didn't send a praise team; he sent a large choir (see 2 Chronicles 20). They had to have been very close in number to the army they were preceding.

The enemy is intimidated by united numbers. It's much harder for him to break through our spiritual barriers when we're many operating as one. That's why he tries so hard to divide us. He wants to reduce us in size in hopes that he can somehow even the odds. In light of this, we must strive to incorporate the choir ministry into our churches whenever possible.

Is There Really Strength in Numbers?

There is a definite place and function for the praise team, but there is also a place (and a definite spiritual advantage) for the choir ministry. A choir singing as one has a strength, in terms of both volume and spirit, that is hard to achieve with just a few singers. I ask you: if the enemy was coming against your church like he came against Jehoshaphat's, would you rather send out ten singers who were united or a hundred singers who were united?

God's Word clearly shows us the advantage of numbers:

> *And ye shall chase your enemies, and they shall fall before you by the sword. And five of you shall chase an hundred, and an hundred of you shall put ten thousand to flight: and your enemies shall fall before you by the sword.*
>
> Leviticus 26:7-8, KJV

Get your choirs organized—for God's glory and for the deliverance of His people.

Review Questions for Chapter 6

1. Just how important is the choir ministry in the church?

_____

2. How does the choir ministry compare with that of a smaller praise team?

_____

3. How many members did David's music ministry have?

_____

4. How many sang in the choir at any one time?

_____

5. What Old Testament scripture best describes the power of numbers?

_____

Points to Ponder for Chapter 6

1. Have I truly appreciated the strength that comes with numbers?

   _____

2. In reference to numbers, have I been satisfied to settle for that which is easier (using smaller worship groups) rather than striving for what is clearly better (organizing a full choir)?

   _____

3. Am I satisfied that I've done what the Lord *"prescribed"* for me and those who work with me in music ministry?

   _____

4. Have I worked toward the type of unity that will intimidate the enemy?

   _____

5. What can I do to promote greater unity among those with whom I work in the church?

   _____

Chapter 7

How To Organize a Choir Ministry

—✦✦✦—

Once the pastor senses the need for a choir ministry, he must first pray for the right leader. If the praise team leader is already teaching vocal parts, he or she may also be able to lead the choir. Whoever the pastor chooses must be a people person with patience. If not, the choir will experience a constant turnover in membership. The person the pastor chooses should have a "corralling" type spirit. This is a gift for gathering together and motivating people for one purpose and goal.

Once the proper leadership is in place, you're ready to organize your church choir. There are four basic steps to organizing a choir ministry. Let's briefly look at each one:

Step 1: The Announcement

In this first step, you want to make the congregation aware that a choir is being formed. You can do this by putting an announcement in your church bulletin, or you can make a special announcement during services. I would do both, just to make certain everyone is notified. Not everyone reads the church bulletin, and someone always misses the announcements during service.

The announcement should be done in such a way as to create excitement. You want the entire church to feel that this new endeavor will enhance the overall ministry of the church. Here is an example of an announcement which would be given by the pastor of the church:

"Many of you have been coming to our services for quite a while now and have been joining with us in our times of praise and worship. Some, perhaps, have enjoyed the singing so much that you've wished, or even prayed, that you could do more. Well, today your prayers have been answered. We're officially starting a choir ministry here at the church. We already have the leadership in place to ensure its success. So, if you feel called to this type of ministry, please come to an initial meeting on the day and month at the time. I really feel that God desires to take us to another level in our

praise and worship to Him, and we need your help to make it happen."

If you put an announcement in the church bulletin or make a separate flier, make it exciting. You don't want the people who read it to think that this is going to be a boring ministry. Allow at least a month of announcements before you have your first meeting. This will ensure that you have informed the majority of the congregation.

Step 2: The Auditions

This is the initial gathering of perspective choir members. I've found that most people are intimidated by the mention of an audition, no matter how talented they may be. You want to reassure everyone that the audition is needed to find out where they are musically.

When the moment arrives, do whatever you can to ease their tensions. One thing that works very well is to have a short time of praise and worship. This will help to get everyone in the right frame of mind and spirit.

After the people have gathered, and you've opened with prayer and praise, you're ready to begin. The first order of business is to have everyone complete a choir member application. On the following page is an example of one I have developed:

CHOIR APPLICATION

Name: _____ Date: _____

Address: _____ City: _____ Zip: _____

Home Phone: ( ) _____ Work Phone: ( ) _____

Birth Date: / / (You must be at least 18 years of age.)

Marital Status: Single Married

Children: Yes No Ages _____

Are you currently a member of the church? _____

How long? _____

If not, how long have you been a regular attender here? _____

Are you presently enrolled in the membership class? _____

Please check one. Your answer does not automatically disqualify you from being a member of the choir.

1. Have you received Jesus as Lord and Savior?   Yes   No

2. Have you received the Baptism of the Holy Spirit?   Yes   No

3. Have you kept yourself from using alcoholic beverages,
   tobacco products, or illegal drugs for the past 12 months?   Yes   No

4. Have you kept yourself from immoral sexual activity such
   as fornication, adultery, incest, or homosexuality for the
   past 12 months?   Yes   No

5. Have you needed any special counseling in the last 12 months?   Yes   No

What vocal part do you sing?   Soprano   Alto   Tenor   Bass

What instrument, if any, do you play? _____

How long? _____

Briefly summarize your musical background? _____
_____
_____
_____

Why do you want to be a part of the music ministry? _____
_____
_____
_____
_____

There are many reasons for this type of application. First, it will help you with the audition process. You will want to make notes on the application regarding the applicant's singing ability. Answers to certain questions will give you an idea of the applicant's motives and where they are spiritually. It will also identify any major issues in their life that might hinder their ability to minister effectively.

Yes, the applicants could lie, but the truth has a way of manifesting itself, and you have the Holy Spirit to help you detect falsehoods.

Once everyone has completed the application, you're ready to audition them one at a time. I suggest that you do this in a separate room if possible. This way, the applicant is less distracted.

The actual audition can be as simple or complicated as you want it to be, depending on what type of choir you're trying to assemble. If your choir members will be required to sight read, then your audition will need to include a sight reading test, in addition to hearing their tonal quality, vocal range, and ability to match tones. If you simply want choir members who can sing what they hear, and also harmonize, your audition process will be simpler.

Most of the choirs I have dealt with have not been required to have the ability to sight read, although we may at times teach that skill. So I usually have the choir applicant sing a simple praise song. This allows me the opportunity to hear everything I need in order to make a fair decision. I also make them harmonize with me, to make sure they can stay on their vocal part.

You should be able to audition the applicants within five minutes each, but don't be rushed. Don't be afraid to make suggestions to an applicant, or even have them sing something two or three times. You want to make sure you hear enough to make a fair decision.

Remember to make notes on the application, so when you review the applications later you don't have to try to remember what an applicant sounded like. You could also record each audition with a small recorder.

Don't feel obligated to tell an applicant right after their audition whether or not they've passed. Tell them you will contact them as soon as a decision has been made. You want enough time to prayerfully consider every applicant.

Once you've done this, you can invite those choir members who have successfully passed the audition to the first official choir rehearsal. Those applicants who did not pass also need to be contacted. Have a one-on-one meeting with them and explain to them the reasons for your decision.

Step 3: The Rehearsals

Once you've assembled the people whom you feel will best serve in this ministry, you're ready to start your initial rehearsals. It's at this time that you'll want to set forth your choir guidelines. This should include information regarding choir officers, rehearsal schedules, and choir uniforms.

You'll also want to hand out any other useful materials that will help your choir members to be more effective in their ministry. You might even want to give them a copy of this book. Some kind of choir packet works great because it makes the choir member feel like they're a part of something special.

Included at the end of the choir guidelines I currently use is a Statement of Agreement, which is a commitment each choir member makes to the Lord regarding their participation in the choir ministry. Here's an example:

Choir Ministry Statement of Agreement

Having read the requirements and procedures of the music department, I, _____ _____ make a commitment of my person, time, and talent to serve as a member of the choir ministry. In making this commitment, I have resolved in my spirit that:

1. *I am called by God and led by His Spirit to be involved in the music ministry of this church.*
2. *I will submit myself to the leadership, policies, and procedures of the music department.*
3. *I am committed to the leadership, vision, and work of this church.*
4. *I will attend all scheduled rehearsals and services, to the best of my ability.*
5. *I will continually pray for the music department, its leadership, and my fellow choir members.*

_____   _____
Signature   Date

This commitment is between the choir member and God. Therefore, while we do ask them to sign it, we don't require them to return it to us. It's a reminder to them of their pledge and commitment to God to be faithful in the ministry to which they feel called.

During rehearsals, you want to teach new music material. You also want to set a target date for the choir's debut. Make sure the entire church knows about this special day.

Step 4: The Choir Debut

All of the hard work, the auditions, the training, and the rehearsals were to musically and spiritually prepare the choir for this day. This is the official public beginning for your choir ministry. This is an exciting day, and here are some helpful suggestions to ensure that it is most effective:

1. Make sure you announce the target debut date during the first official rehearsal. This gives the choir something to work toward. It also gives them a chance to invite their family and friends.

2. You definitely want the choir to be in some type of uniform for their debut. So, decide during the first few rehearsals what the choir's attire will be. (Remember, this includes inward as well as outward preparation.) Give the choir

members plenty of time to get the uniform you decide on.

3. Have the pastor introduce the choir when it's time for them to sing. This reassures the congregation that the pastor is in full support of this new ministry.

4. Have a brief dedication ceremony in which the pastor publicly prays for the choir and formally dedicates them into the service of the Lord.

5. Have a choir reception following the debut service to celebrate the occasion.

Once this day is over, you're on your way. Continue to do what you can to keep excitement in the choir. Try to have a new song to teach them at least every other rehearsal.

Also, do whatever it takes to keep a spirit of unity in the choir. Choir fellowships and periodic outings work great. The collective effort a choir puts forth during the week to be both musically and spiritually prepared will directly reflect on how effective they are when they minister.

Review Questions for Chapter 7

1. What are the four basic steps for organizing a choir?

   a. _____

   b. _____

   c. _____

   d. _____

2. Who is the one person a pastor must prayerfully choose himself if the choir is to be successful?

   _____

Points to Ponder for Chapter 7

1. Have I prayed enough about any decision I must make in relationship to the music ministry of the church?

_____

2. Is the music ministry as exciting to me as it should be or as it once was?

_____

3. Am I constantly working to improve myself so that I can do my best for God in this ministry?

_____

4. Am I willing to give my time to this worthwhile ministry, without reservation?

_____

5. Can I say that I'm in agreement with the principles laid out in the Choir Ministry Statement of Agreement?

_____

Chapter 8

From My Heart to Every Part

——◆◆◆——

In this chapter, I would like to share some final thoughts concerning the four major parts which make up the music ministry. My heart's desire is for the music ministry, for which you are called, to become all that God originally intended it to be.

The music ministry in any church is made up of four very important parts. They are:

1.   The Senior Pastor

2.   The Music Director (or Minister of Music)

3.   The Singers (Choir Members)

4.   The Musicians

Each of the above, individually or collectively, can make a vast difference in the overall effectiveness of a music ministry. If any of these parts fail to understand God's purpose for music in the temple, the ministry will probably experience mediocrity and spiritual defeat. Therefore, in this closing chapter, I have penned a personal letter from my heart to each part. I pray that God will speak to your heart as you read the letter that pertains to you and that you will truly understand God's purpose for the music ministry in your church.

Dear Senior Pastor:

A writer once said, "The ideal role of the pastor in church music is one where the pastor provides leadership in service objectives, mutually arrives at overall goals or objectives for the music program with the minister of music, and functions in the role of counselor to the minister of music." [16] The vision and purpose of the music program should be directly related to your corporate vision for the church. It's your responsibility to make sure that this vision is adequately communicated to your music director, as it relates to the music of the church. This will determine the direction the music program takes in terms of music styles, song selection, types of choirs and instruments.

Although you may not be a musician or singer, you need to be able to communicate to your minister of music the type of praise and worship and choir songs you prefer. This can be accomplished by simply giving the music director some examples on CD.

Music sets the tone and atmosphere in the services, and you must agree with the tone that's being set. Open communication between the minister of music and yourself is critical.

One of the most critical decisions you'll ever make concerning your church is who you choose to be your minister of music. This person is usually in front of the congregation just as much as you are. Therefore, the person you select can be either a great blessing to your church or a spiritual detriment. Don't settle for anything less than God's standards for a minister of music.

You should never appoint a music director who has a musical preference, or style, contrary to what you desire, and you should always feel free to make suggestions about specific songs you want ministered. At the same time, you should allow the music director a certain amount of freedom to express his or her ideas and gifts within the bounds of the corporate vision. "If a pastor is the right kind of pastor, he wants the minister of music to know how to meet the spiritual needs of people through music." [17]

Finally, I caution you not to make the same mistake King David made when he initially decided to bring the Ark back to Jerusalem. After that first disastrous attempt, he gave the main reason for his failure:

> We did not inquire of him [the Lord] about how to do it in the prescribed way.
>
> 1 Chronicles 15:13

It is my prayer that you will consistently inquire of the Lord about how to usher His presence into your services and that you will have a clear revelation as to the major role the music ministry plays in achieving this goal.

Dear Music Director:

God has not only called you, but He has also chosen you to plan and administer the entire music program of the church you attend. This, of course, includes the oversight of one or more choirs, the band, and perhaps a praise team. As minister of music, it is your responsibility to make sure that the music program is going in the direction prescribed by you and the pastor of the church.

Always remember that you work for and report to your pastor. The pastor is the final authority on the music of his church. He has the right to reject the use of a song, even if you don't agree with his reasoning. A pastor also has the right to suggest that a certain song be taught to the choir or band. Maybe he heard it on radio or television or at a church he was visiting.

The pastor may want to be informed of any new songs you're planning to teach to the choir and congregation. As the pastor, he has that right, and it is essential that communication from him be welcomed by you at all times.

Encompassed in the many abilities of a leader is the ability to care and serve. You're not simply one who can teach songs, play an instrument, or conduct a choir. You're a servant. I've found that a great percentage of what I do as a minister of music has nothing to do with music at all. Singers and musicians have many of the same serious needs and concerns as people in the congregation. The most important thing you can do for them is to show genuine concern for their needs. This is the only way you can earn the privilege of being followed.

Choir members don't want or need a dictator, and the authority you have been given should never be abused. They need a leader with the attributes and characteristics of Christ. They don't need someone who will talk at them, but rather talk with them.

Each member of the choir is looking for a sense of belonging and significance. They may never say it, but they want to know that the small part they're contributing is not only special, but appreciated. And it should be.

Finally, as a minister of music, you, no doubt, are very talented. You're most likely held in high esteem by your pastor, congregation, choir, and band members, in much the same way as Lucifer was in heaven. I encourage and also warn you in the name of the Lord not to make the same mistakes he made. You cannot live just any kind of lifestyle and expect God to be pleased with your praise. And neither can you truly succeed on just the "outward adorning" of your gift.

Your special talents and gifts are nothing without the anointing of God. And the anointing or approval of God will require much more of you than just a song and dance. It will require that you live a life yielded to the lordship of Christ on a daily basis.

It is my deepest prayer for you that you will not be thrown off track by the many compliments and accolades you will receive, and that you will remain humble, always realizing that every good and perfect gift comes from the Father above.

Dear Singers:

You are the special ones whom God has specifically chosen and set aside for the purpose of ministering unto Him in the Holy Place. God has given you as a gift to the pastor of your church. You don't just have the spirit of praise; you also possess the spirit of Levi.

You have been given the awesome responsibility of singing forth the truth. You are spiritually going before your pastor with praises and shouts of deliverance in order to make the ground fertile for the Word he or she will deliver. But remember, you cannot sing forth the truth unless you are operating in truth with one another.

As choir members, you're an extension of the congregation, in that you were congregational members first before you became choir members. In that sense, the congregation easily relates to you and will even tend to mimic you during church services.

You must always be aware that you're an example. If the choir doesn't clap, the congregation probably won't clap. If you don't smile and look excited, the congregation probably won't respond to your ministry. Generally speaking, a dead choir produces a dead congregation, but a vibrant choir excites those in attendance. You must always sing with fervency, realizing that you're actually prophesying to God's people in song (see 1 Chronicles 25:1).

Your ability to sing doesn't automatically qualify you to become a choir member if you haven't met God's requirements. You must also have a sincere desire to minister unto the Lord in song and be willing to be trained in order to maximize your musical potential.

Many people join choirs for the wrong reasons, and this causes major problems with both leadership and fellow choir members. The usual result is that there will be more than one vision (division) in the choir.

Some people join a choir because of its social value. Others join because they have a hidden agenda to get in the spotlight. The only reason one should become a part of the choir ministry is because they feel called to that particular ministry.

Finally, always remember that God chose you based on what He invested in you musically and your willingness to serve. Being a choir member is, therefore, a privilege, not a right. Don't take your ministry for granted. Make sure you're in your place at the prescribed time so that the service of the Lord can go as planned (see 2 Chronicles 35:15-16).

It is my sincere prayer that God will reward you for the countless hours you've given and will continue to sacrifice for the sake of this ministry. I pray that He will multiply it all back to you in the ways you need it most. I pray that you will have a renewed understanding regarding your ministry, and that He will anoint you afresh from this day forward.

Dear Musicians:

The word musician is taken from the word muse, which means "to consider thoughtfully, ponder or meditate." [18] As a musician, you're called to provide accompaniment for the singers. Your music sets the atmosphere, or mood, through which the words of a song will travel to the listener's heart. If the music is distracting, the message will not be effectively communicated.

In many of the scriptures that we have read regarding choirs, the musicians were right there with the singers. The scripture that really makes this point clear is found in Second Chronicles:

> The trumpeters and singers joined in unison, as with one voice, to give praise and thanks to the LORD. Accompanied by trumpets, cymbals and other instruments, they raised their voices in praise to the LORD and sang: "He is good; his love endures forever." Then the temple of the LORD was filled with a cloud, and the priests could not perform their service because of the cloud, for the glory of the LORD filled the temple of God.
>
> 2 Chronicles 5:13-14

It's very clear from this passage that the deciding factor for the manifestation of God's glory was the fact that the musicians and singers were ministering as one. The musicians were not trying to drown out the choir, nor were they so busy trying to play individual solos that they missed their cues.

You must never consider yourselves separate from or superior to the choir. The two must work together in perfect unity, as one. Otherwise, you will never experience the true manifestation of God's glory.

Being a musician is a priestly office of ministry, and, because of that, you must be careful to live a godly life. God will not settle for good musicians who have unclean lifestyles.

My prayer for you is that you will listen for the music and melodies of heaven rather than imitate the music of the world. Be open to God's musical will for your life. Spend time with Him, and allow Him to speak to the heartstrings of your soul.

Blessings to all of you who labor in the temple of the Lord.

Review Questions for Chapter 8

1. What are the four important parts that make up the music ministry of any church?

   a. _____

   b. _____

   c. _____

   d. _____

2. What is the ideal role of the pastor in church music?

   _____

Points to Ponder for Chapter 8

1. Am I doing my part to make the ministry of my church successful?

_____

2. Am I guilty of David's mistake, not inquiring of the Lord concerning His prescribed way of doing things?

_____

3. Am I fully submitted to my pastor?

_____

4. Do I keep others informed when it is required or even desirable?

_____

5. Am I sensitive to the personal needs of the other musicians/singers with whom I minister?

_____

Endnotes

───❖───

1. James Strong, LL.D, S.T.D., *The New Strong's Exhaustive Concordance of the Bible* (Nashville, TN: Thomas Nelson Publishers, 1990), Dictionary of the Hebrew Bible, p. 47.

2. *Ibid.*, p. 59.

3. Strong, *Strong's Exhaustive Concordance*, Dictionary of the Hebrew Bible, p.52.

4. *Ibid.*, p. 89.

5. Funk & Wagnalls, *New International Dictionary of the English Language* (Newark, NJ: Publishers International Press, 1984), p. 234.

6. *Ibid.*, p. 111.

7. Strong, *Strong's Exhaustive Concordance*, Dictionary of the Hebrew Bible, pp. 114, 115.

8. *Ibid.*, p. 114

9. Strong, *Strong's Exhaustive Concordance*, Dictionary of the Greek Testament, p.12.

10. *Ibid.*, p. 72

11. Funk & Wagnalls, *New International Dictionary*, p. 1324

12. Strong, *Strong's Exhaustive Concordance*, Dictionary of the Greek Testament, p. 9; and Funk & Wagnalls, *New International Dictionary*, p. 1348.

13. Herbert Lockyer, Sr., *Nelson's Illustrated Bible Dictionary*, (Nashville, TN: Thomas Nelson Publishers, 1986) p. 657.

14. Strong, *Strong's Exhaustive Concordance*, Dictionary of the Hebrew Bible, p. 33.

15. *Ibid.*, p. 89.

16. Robert Berglund, *A Philosophy of Church Music* (Chicago, IL: Moody Press, 1985), p. 83.

17. William L. Hooper, *Ministry & Musicians* (Nashville, TN: Broadman Press, 1986), p. 110.

18. Funk & Wagnalls, *New International Dictionary*, p. 837.